BOB CHILCOTT

The Angry Planet

An Environmental Cantata

CONTENTS

1a. 6pm
(Choir 1, Choir 2) *page* 1

1b. As if
(Chamber Choir) 10

1c. Yellow Eye
(Children's Choir, Choir 2) 15

2a. Remember
(Chamber Choir, Choir 1) 21

2b. 9pm
(Choir 1, Choir 2) 32

2c. Green Rain
(Children' s Choir, Choir 1) 45

3a. Midnight
(Soprano Solo, Choir 1, Choir 2) 53

3b. We need
(Chamber Choir) 63

3c. 3am
(Choir 1, Choir 2) 67

3d. Sorry too late
(Chamber Choir, Choir 1, Choir 2) 84

4a. Peppermint freckles
(Children's Choir, Chamber Choir) 94

4b. 6am (Lutra lutra)
(Choir 1) 102

4c. Perhaps
(Children's Choir, Chamber Choir, Choir 1, Choir 2) 109

MUSIC DEPARTMENT

The Angry Planet was commissioned by David Hill and the Bach Choir.

The premiere was given by a choir of primary school children from West London, the BBC Singers, the Bach Choir, and the National Youth Choir of Great Britain. The performance took place on 4 August 2012 at the Royal Albert Hall in London, as part of the 2012 BBC Proms.

Performance Notes

The Angry Planet is a large-scale cantata on the theme of the environment.
The piece has been designed for a large children's choir, a chamber choir, and two large mixed choirs.
The work has been written in four main movements, each one dividing into sections of different scorings.

Scoring

Children's Choir (optional divisi)

Chamber Choir (SATB)

Large Choir 1 (SATB)

Large Choir 2 (SATB)

Duration : *c.*45 minutes

The Angry Planet

1a

6pm

Charles Bennett

BOB CHILCOTT

Printed in Great Britain

OXFORD UNIVERSITY PRESS, MUSIC DEPARTMENT, GREAT CLARENDON STREET, OXFORD OX2 6DP

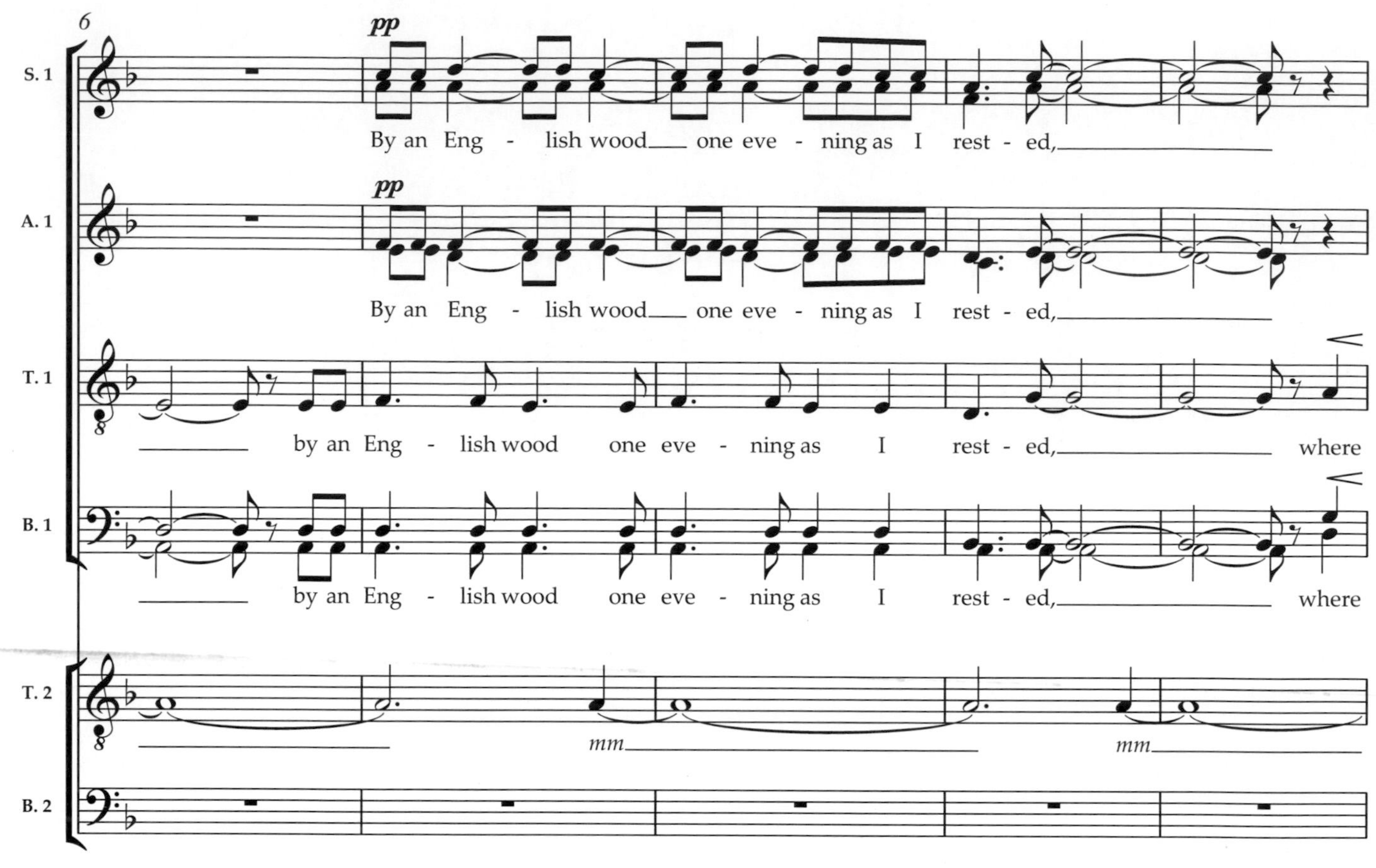

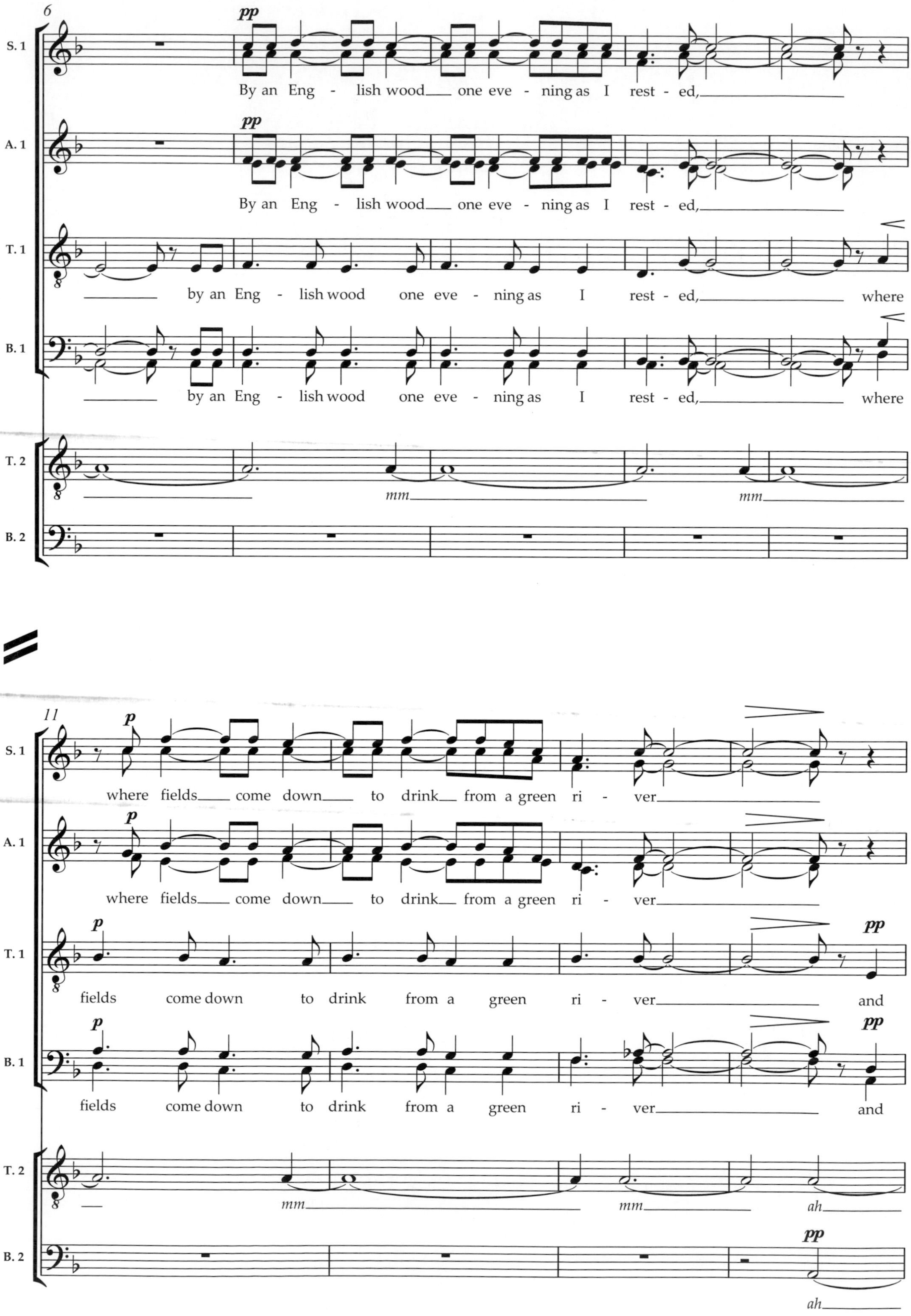
6
S. 1
pp
By an Eng - lish wood one eve - ning as I rest - ed,
A. 1
pp
By an Eng - lish wood one eve - ning as I rest - ed,
T. 1
by an Eng - lish wood one eve - ning as I rest - ed, where
B. 1
by an Eng - lish wood one eve - ning as I rest - ed, where
T. 2
mm
mm
B. 2
11
S. 1
p
where fields come down to drink from a green ri - ver
A. 1
p
where fields come down to drink from a green ri - ver
T. 1
p
fields come down to drink from a green ri - ver
pp
and
B. 1
p
fields come down to drink from a green ri - ver
pp
and
T. 2
mm
mm
ah
B. 2
pp
ah

15
S. 1
pp
and black - birds bring the dark in with their song,
A. 1
pp
and black - birds bring the dark in with their song,
T. 1
black - birds bring the dark in with their song,
B. 1
black - birds bring the dark in with their song,
S. 2
p
ah ah
pp
A. 2
p
ah ah
pp
T. 2
ah mm
B. 2
ah
19
S. 1
p cresc.
a slen-der-ness swayed and curved of its own ac - cord like a
A. 1
p cresc.
a slen-der-ness swayed and curved of its own ac - cord like a
T. 1
p cresc.
a slen - der-ness swayed and curved of its own ac-cord
B. 1
p cresc.
a slen - der - ness swayed and curved like a
T. 2

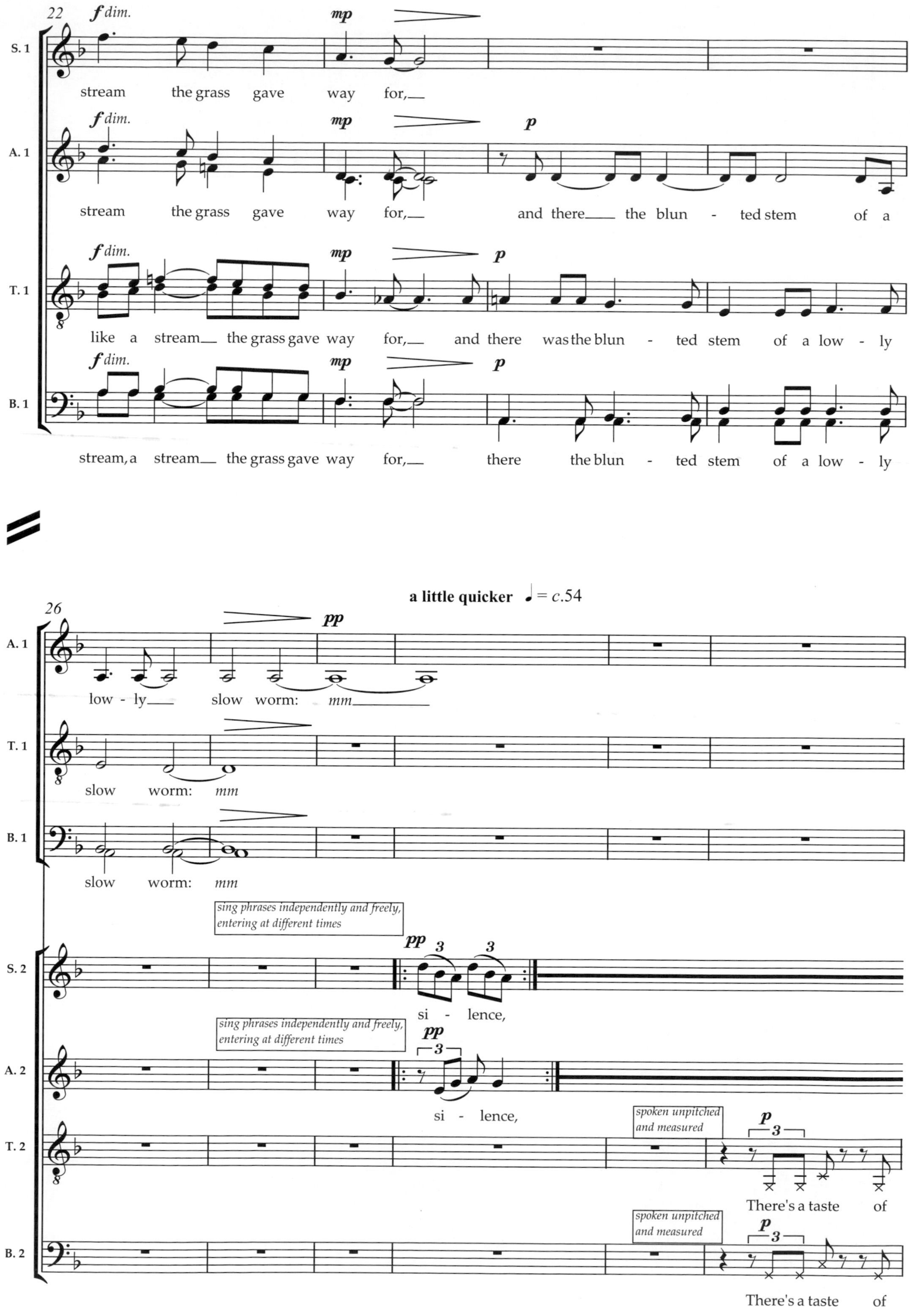

26

a little quicker ♩ = c.54

A. 1
pp
low - ly slow worm: mm

T. 1
slow worm: mm

B. 1
slow worm: mm

sing phrases independently and freely, entering at different times

S. 2
pp
si - lence,

sing phrases independently and freely, entering at different times

A. 2
pp
si - lence,

spoken unpitched and measured

T. 2
p
There's a taste of

spoken unpitched and measured

B. 2
p
There's a taste of

32
S. 2
A. 2
T. 2
B. 2
si - lence,
si - lence,
si - lence,
si - lence,
si - lence,
si - lence,
si-lence in the grass, like a win-ter we ne-ver wake up from, where
si-lence in the grass, like a win-ter we ne-ver wake up from, where
35
si - lence,
si - lence,
si - lence,
si - lence,
si - lence,
pp
all the world is emp-tied of us for-ev-er,
pp
all the world is emp-tied of us for - ev-er, for-
38
Tempo primo ♩ = c.48
T. 1
B. 1
mf cresc.
And the
mf cresc.
And the
si - lence,
mf
for-ev-er.
Ah ah
ev - er.

42
S. 1
mf cresc.
f
The field was sud-den-ly thronged with a great crowd,
A. 1
mf cresc.
f
The field was sud-den-ly thronged with a great crowd,
T. 1
f
field was sud-den-ly thronged with a great crowd,
B. 1
f
field was sud-den-ly thronged with a great crowd,
S. 2
mp cresc.
f
The field was sud-den-ly thronged with a great
A. 2
mp cresc.
f
The field was sud-den-ly thronged with a great
T. 2
mp cresc.
f
The field was sud-den-ly thronged with a great
B. 2
mp cresc.
f
The field was sud-den-ly thronged with a great

44
cresc.
ff dim.
S. 1
look-ing for some-thing they'd lost and could not find, and sor - ry, sor - ry,
A. 1
look-ing for some-thing they'd lost and could not find, and sor - ry, sor - ry,
T. 1
look - ing, look - ing for some - thing lost and could not find, and sor - ry, sor - ry,
B. 1
look - ing for some - thing lost and could not find, and sor - ry, sor - ry,
S. 2
crowd, look - ing for some-thing lost, and sor - ry, sor - ry,
A. 2
crowd, look - ing for some-thing lost, and sor - ry, sor - ry,
T. 2
crowd, look - ing for some-thing lost, and sor - ry, sor - ry,
B. 2
crowd, look - ing for some-thing lost, and sor - ry, sor - ry,

46
S. 1
mp
sor - ry too late as al - ways.
A. 1
mp
sor - ry too late as al - ways.
T. 1
mp
pp
sor - ry too late as al - ways, al - ways. mm By an
B. 1
mp
pp
sor - ry too late as al - ways. By an
S. 2
mp
sor - ry too late as al - ways.
A. 2
mp
sor - ry too late as al - ways.
T. 2
mp
pp
sor - ry too late as al - ways. mm
B. 2
mp
sor - ry too late as al - ways.

51
T. 1
Eng - lish wood, by an Eng - lish wood as I
B. 1
Eng - lish wood, by an Eng - lish wood as I
S. 2
pp
(fade)
si - lence, si - lence,
A. 2
pp
3
si - lence, si - lence,
T. 2
mm mm
55
rest - ed, rest - ed,
rest - ed, rest - ed,
si - lence, si - lence,
si - lence, si -
mm mm

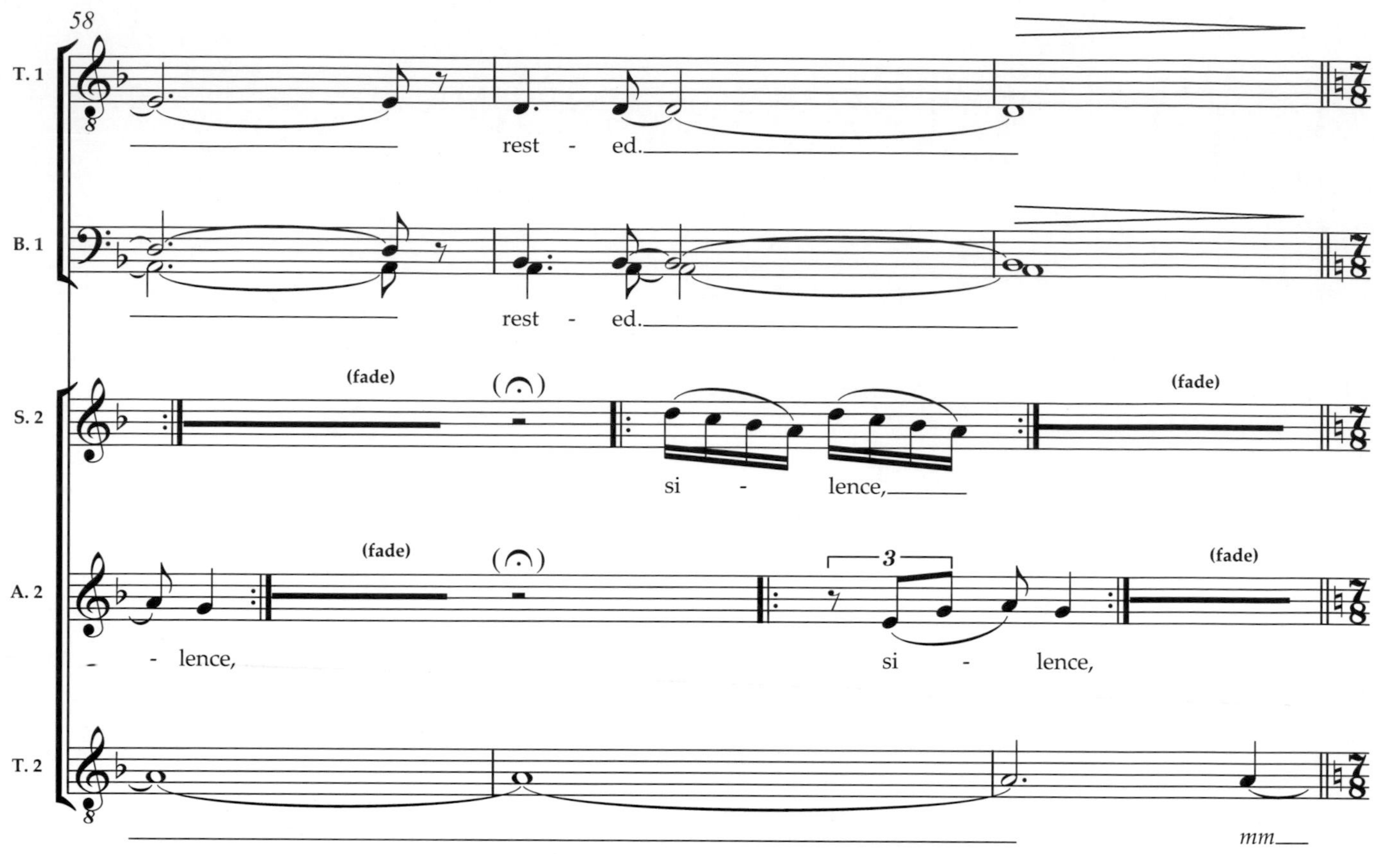
58
T. 1
rest - ed.
B. 1
rest - ed.
S. 2
(fade)
si - lence,
(fade)
A. 2
- lence,
(fade)
3
si - lence,
(fade)
T. 2
mm

1b
As if

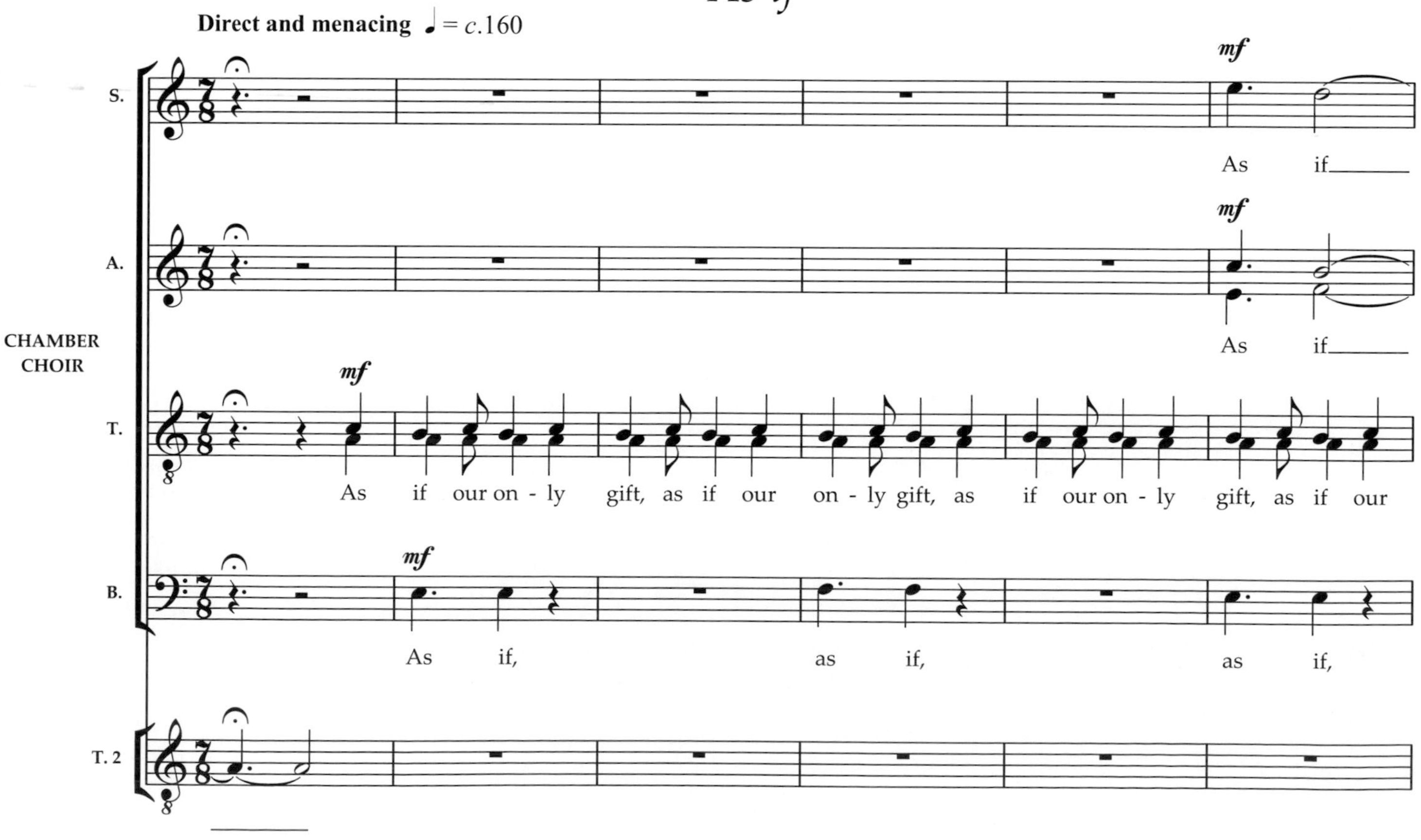
Direct and menacing ♩ = c.160
CHAMBER CHOIR
S.
mf
As if
A.
mf
As if
T.
mf
As if our on - ly gift, as if our on - ly gift, as if our on - ly gift, as if our
B.
mf
As if, as if, as if,
T. 2

7
S.
A.
T.
B.
our on - ly gift is to break and shat - ter and crush, break and shat - ter and
our on - ly gift is to break and shat - ter and crush, break and shat - ter and
on - ly gift, as if, as if our on - ly gift to break, shat - ter and crush, to break and shat - ter and
as if, break, shat - ter and crush, to break and shat - ter and

13
S.
A.
T.
B.
crush; as if our on - ly gift is to break and shat - ter and
crush; as if our on - ly gift is to break and shat - ter and
crush; as if our on - ly gift, as if our on - ly gift, our on - ly gift, to break, shat - ter and
crush; as if our on - ly gift, as if our on - ly gift, our on - ly gift, to break, shat - ter and

19
S.
A.
T.
B.
ff
f
crush, break and shat - ter and crush; and rip the hedge-row out, as
crush, break and shat - ter and crush; and rip the hedge-row out, as
crush, break and shat - ter and crush; to grub the or - chard up and rip the hedge, the hedge-row
crush, to break and shat - ter and crush; to grub the or - chard up and rip the hedge, the hedge-row
24
if they were a curse, as if they were a curse, as if they were a curse, as if they were a curse, as
if, as if, as if,
out, as if they
out, as if they
30
if, as if they were a curse or else a blight as if they were un - sight - ly, or
as if, else a blight as if they were un - sight - ly, or
were a curse, a curse, or else a blight as if they were un -
were a curse, a curse, or else a blight as if they were un -

36
S.
A.
T.
B.
ff
else a blight as if they were un - sight - ly, un - sight - ly, un -
or else a blight as if they were un - sight - ly, un -
-sight - ly,
42
f
-sight - ly:
haul its root a -
haul,
we have come to hack the tree of Eng - land down,
haul its
we have come to hack the tree of Eng -
49
dim.
poco rit.
a little slower
p
-way, a - way.
To - night we'll be
haul its root a - way and sell it for fire - wood.
- way, a - way, a - way and sell it for fire - wood. To - night
root, haul its root a - way
- land down, and sell it for fire - wood. To - night

57
Tempo primo
S.
warm,— warm.— To-
A.
warm,— warm.— To-
T.
— we'll be warm,— as if our on - ly gift, as if our on - ly gift, as if our on - ly
B.
— we'll be warm,— As if, as if,
64
S.
-night we'll be warm— and be - sides— it,— it was al-read-y rot-ten, it was al-read-y
A.
-night we'll be warm— and be - sides— it,— it was al-read-y rot-ten, it was al-read-y
T.
gift, as if our on-ly gift, as if, as if our on-ly gift,— it was al-read-y rot-ten, it was al-read-y
B.
as if, as if, it al-read-y rot-ten, it al-read-y
71
pp
S.
rot - ten, it was al - read - y rot - ten, rot - ten.
A.
rot - ten, it was al - read - y rot - ten, rot - ten.
T.
rot - ten, it was al - read - y rot - ten, rot - ten, as if.
B.
rot - ten, it al - read - y rot - ten, rot - ten, if.

1c
Yellow Eye

8
1.
blind, we are dim - pled_ moons or bald old men gone blind.
blind, we are dim - pled_ moons or bald old men gone blind.
S. 2
p
Yel - - low, yel - low eye.
A. 2
yel-low eye, yel - low eye, yel - low eye, eye.
T. 2
yel - low eye, yel - low eye, yel - low eye, eye.
B. 2
yel - low, yel - - low, yel - low eye.
12
1 & 2
mf
We_ point the neat_ ar-rows of our leaves in_
S. 2
ev' - ry - where,
A. 2
ev' ry - where, ev' ry - where, ev'- ry - where, ev' ry - where,
T. 2
ev' - ry - where, ev' - ry - where, ev' - ry - where, ev' - ry - where,
B. 2
ev' - ry - where, ev' - ry - where, ev' - ry - where, ev' - ry - where,

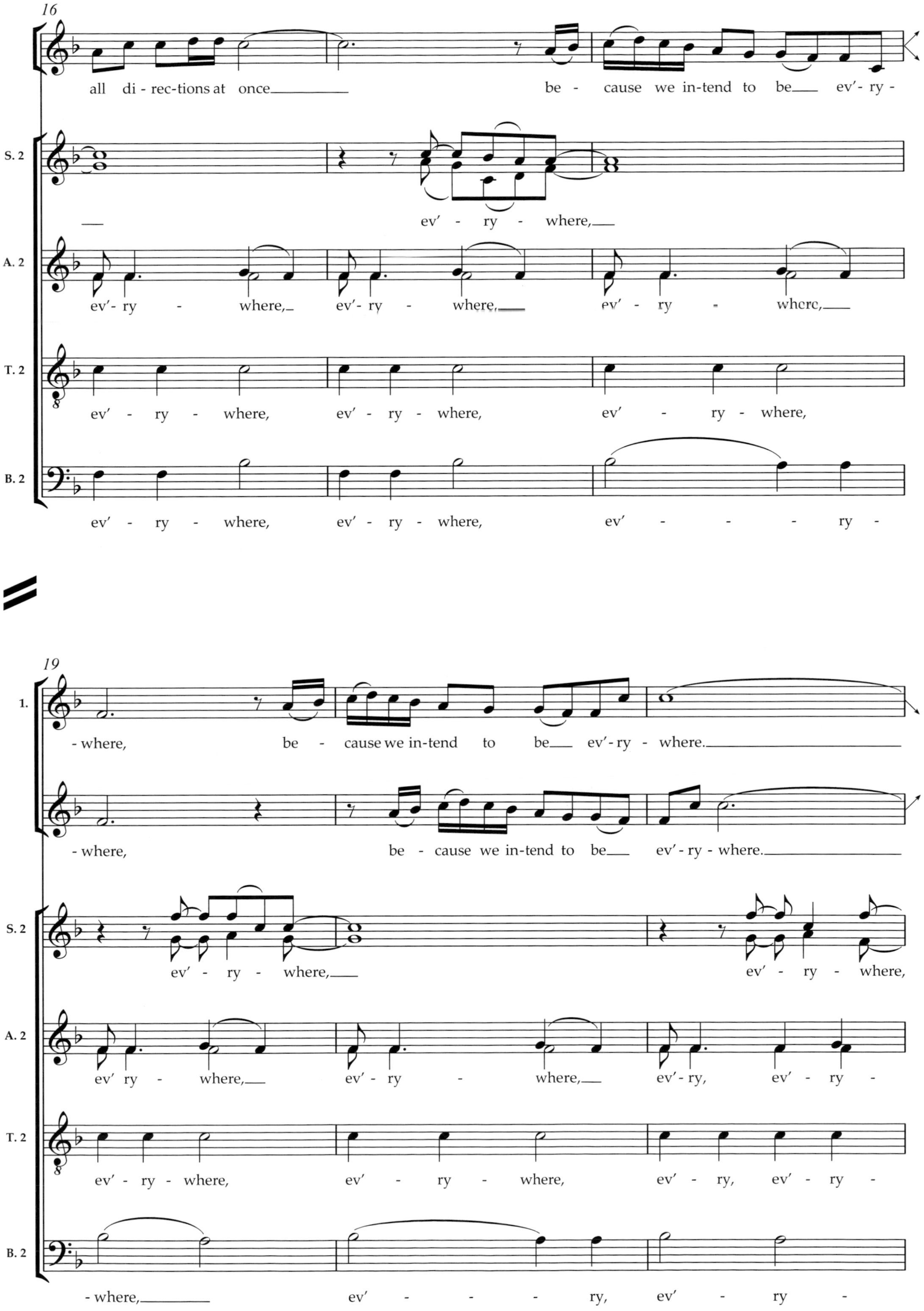

19

1.
- where, be - cause we in-tend to be ev'-ry - where.

- where, be - cause we in-tend to be ev'-ry - where.

S. 2
ev' - ry - where, ev' - ry - where,

A. 2
ev' ry - where, ev'-ry - where, ev'-ry, ev' - ry -

T. 2
ev'-ry-where, ev' - ry - where, ev' - ry, ev' - ry -

B. 2
- where, ev' - - - - ry, ev' - ry -

22

1&2 — Our roots go down to the first days of Earth, we flew_ our_ seeds be-

S. 2 — *mp* go down,

A. 2 - where._ *mp* roots go down, roots go down,

T. 2 - where._ *mp* roots go down,_ roots go down,

B. 2 *mp* roots go down, roots go down,
- where._ go_ down, roots go down,

25

fore the in- ven - tion of birds. Al - though you do not like us we are

S. 2 — roots_ go down,_

A. 2 roots go down, down, here to stay,

T. 2 roots go down,_ roots go down, here to stay,_

B. 2 roots go down, roots go down, here to stay,
go_ down, go down, to_ stay,

28
here to stay. In time we shall grow o - ver you com - plete - ly.
S. 2
to stay, here to stay.
A. 2
here to stay, here to stay, stay,
T. 2
here to stay, here to stay, here to stay,
here to stay, here to stay, here to stay,
B. 2
here to stay, to stay, to stay,
31
mf
We o - pen a yel-low eye in - to the
S. 2
A. 2
p
stay. Yel-low eye, yel-low eye, yel-low eye,
T. 2
p
stay. Yel - low eye, yel - low eye, yel - low eye,
B. 2
stay.
35
sun, When our lash - es blow a - way we are
A. 2
yel - low eye, yel - low eye, yel - low eye,
T. 2
yel - low eye, yel - low eye, yel - low eye,

38
1.
dim - pled moons or bald old men gone blind,
we are dim - pled moons or bald old men gone
dim - pled moons or bald old men gone blind,
we are dim - pled moons or bald old
S. 2
p
Yel - low,
A. 2
yel - low eye, yel-low eye, yel - low eye,
T. 2
yel - low eye, yel - low eye, yel - low eye,
p
B. 2
Yel - low, yel - low, yel - - low,
41
1.
blind.
men gone blind.
S. 2
yel - low eye.
A. 2
yel - low eye, eye. Yel - low eye,
T. 2
yel - low eye, eye. Yel - low eye,
B. 2
yel - low eye.

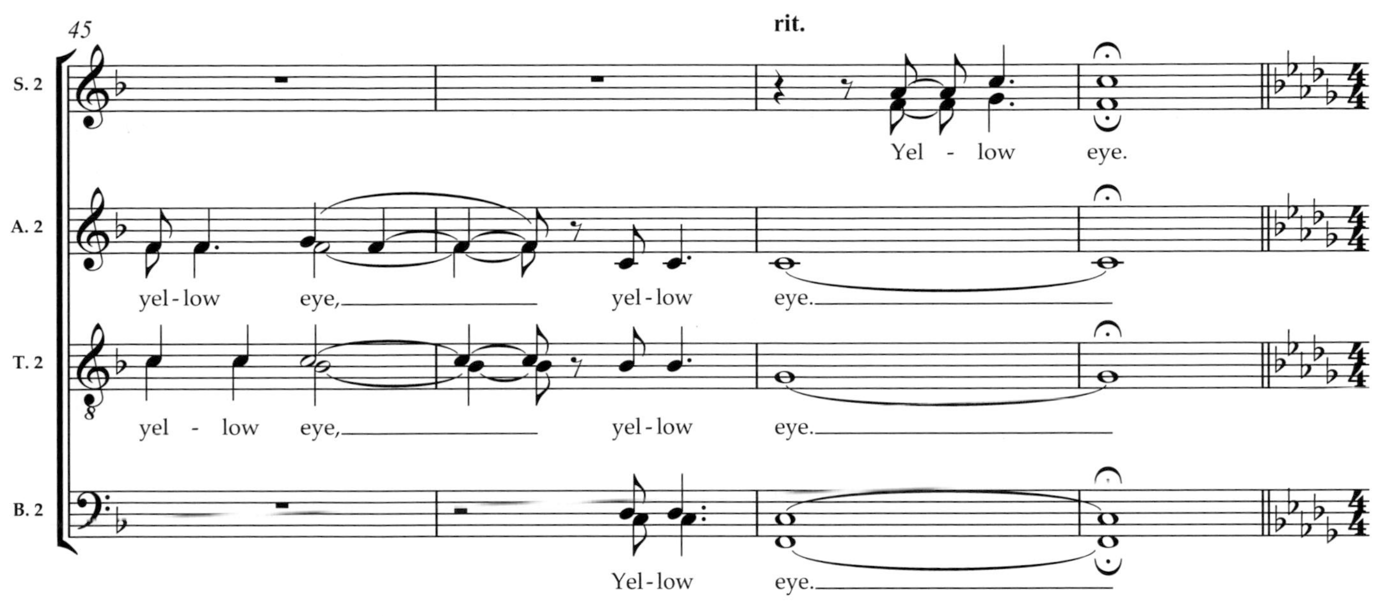

2a
Remember

Hushed and expressive ♩ = *c.*63

CHAMBER CHOIR

S. *pp* Re-

A. *pp* Re-

T. *pp* Re-

B. *pp* Re-

CHOIR 1

S. 1 *pp* Re - mem-ber, re - mem - ber, re - mem-ber, re - mem - ber,

A. 1 *pp* Re - mem-ber, re - mem - ber, re - mem-ber, re - mem - ber,

T. 1 *pp* Re - mem - ber, re - mem - ber, re - mem - ber,

B. 1 *pp* Re - mem - ber, re - mem - ber, re - mem - ber,

7
S.
-mem - ber those is - lands, re - mem - ber those is - lands, those is - lands the
A.
-mem - ber those is - lands, re - mem - ber those is - lands, those is - lands the
T.
-mem - ber those is - lands, re - mem - ber those is - lands, those is - lands the
B.
-mem - ber those is - lands, re - mem - ber those is - lands, those is - lands the
S. 1
re - mem - ber, re - mem - ber,
A. 1
re - mem - ber, re - mem - ber,
T. 1
re - mem - ber, re - mem - ber,
B. 1
re - mem - ber, re - mem - ber,

14
S.
pp
poco cresc.
mp
waves washed o - ver? Where were they? Where were they?
A.
pp
poco cresc.
mp
waves washed o - ver? Where were they? Where were they?
T.
pp
poco cresc.
mp
waves washed o - ver? Where were they? Where were they?
B.
pp
poco cresc.
mp
waves washed o - ver? Where were they? Where were they?
S. 1
pp
poco cresc.
mp
re - mem - ber. Where were they? Where
A. 1
pp
poco cresc.
mp
re - mem - ber. Where were they? Where
T. 1
pp
poco cresc.
mp
re - mem - ber. Where were they? Where
B. 1
pp
poco cresc.
mp
re - mem - ber. Where were they? Where

20
S.
mf dolce
dim.
Can you re - mem - ber? Can you re - mem - ber, re - mem - ber?
A.
mf dolce
dim.
Can you re - mem - ber? Can you re - mem - ber, re - mem - ber?
T.
mf dolce
dim.
Can you re - mem - ber? Can you re - mem - ber, re - mem - ber?
B.
mf dolce
dim.
Can you re - mem - ber? Can you re - mem - ber, re - mem - ber?
S. 1
mf dolce
dim.
were they? Re - mem - ber, re - mem - ber, re - mem - ber?
A. 1
mf dolce
dim.
were they? Re - mem - ber, re - mem - ber, re - mem - ber, re - mem - ber?
T. 1
mf dolce
dim.
were they? Re - mem - ber, re - mem - ber, re - mem - ber, re - mem - ber?
B. 1
mf dolce
dim.
were they? Re - mem - ber, re - mem - ber, re - mem - ber?

poco più mosso
27
S.
A.
T.
B.
S. 1
A. 1
T. 1
B. 1
p cresc.
mf cresc.
What hap-pened to those who lived there? What hap-pened to
What hap-pened to those who lived there? What hap-pened to
What hap-pened to those who lived there? What hap-pened to those who
What hap-pened to those who lived there, lived there, who

31

S. *f* — *ff*
heads, our
those there? It's wa - ter un-der the bridge. It's wa - ter o - ver our heads,

A. *f* — *ff*
heads,
those there? It's wa - ter un - der, un-der the bridge. It's wa - ter o - ver, o-ver our heads, our

T. *f* — *ff*
lived there? It's wa - ter un - der, un-der the bridge. It's wa - ter o - ver, o-ver our heads, our

B. *f* — *ff*
lived there? It's wa - ter un-der the bridge. It's wa - ter o - ver our heads, our

36

poco rit. **Tempo primo**

S. heads,
dim. *mp*
o - ver our heads, o - ver our heads. A land that's drowned for -

A. o - ver our heads, o - ver our heads.
dim. *mp*
heads, o - ver our heads. A land that's drowned for -

T. *dim.* *mp*
heads, o - ver our heads, our heads. Land

B. heads, our heads, our heads.
dim. *mp*
heads, o - ver our heads. Land

40
S.
pp
-ev - er, a land that's drowned for - ev - er, for - ev - er,
A.
pp
-ev - er, a land that's drowned for - ev - er, for - ev - er,
T.
pp
drowned, land drowned for - ev - er,
B.
pp
drowned, land drowned for - ev - er,
S. 1
pp
Re - mem - ber, re - mem - ber,
A. 1
pp
Re - mem - ber, re - mem - ber,
T. 1
pp
Re - mem - ber, re -
B. 1
pp
Re - mem - ber, re -

45
S.
A.
T.
B.
p dolce
for - ev - er.
If we on - ly had a ra - ven we could
S. 1
A. 1
T. 1
B. 1
re - mem - ber, re - mem - ber,
-mem - ber, re - mem - ber,
re - mem - ber,

52
S.
A.
T.
B.
S. 1
A. 1
T. 1
B. 1
mp
p
send him out until he came back with an oak leaf. If we on - ly had a
send him out until he came back with an oak leaf. If we on - ly had a
send him out until he came back with an oak leaf. If we on - ly had a
send him out until he came back with an oak leaf. If we on - ly had a
re - mem - ber, re - mem - ber,
re - mem - ber, re - mem - ber,
re - mem - ber, re - mem - ber,
re - mem - ber, re - mem - ber,

59
S.
pp
dove, a dove.
A.
pp
dove, a dove.
T.
pp
dove, a dove.
B.
pp
dove, a dove.
S. 1
pp
re - mem - ber, re - mem - ber, re - mem-ber, re - mem - ber,
A. 1
pp
re - mem - ber, re - mem - ber, re - mem-ber, re - mem - ber,
T. 1
pp
re - mem - ber, re - mem - ber, re - mem - ber, re -
B. 1
pp
re - mem - ber, re - mem - ber, re - mem - ber, re -

rit.
65
S.
pp
ppp
Re-mem - ber, re - mem - ber.
A.
pp
ppp
Re-mem - ber, re - mem - ber.
T.
pp
ppp
Re-mem - ber, re - mem - ber.
B.
pp
ppp
Re-mem - ber, re - mem - ber.
S. 1
ppp
re - mem-ber, re - mem - ber, re - mem - ber.
A. 1
ppp
re - mem-ber, re - mem - ber, re - mem - ber.
T. 1
ppp
-mem - ber, re - mem - ber, re - mem - ber.
B. 1
ppp
-mem - ber, re - mem - ber, re - mem - ber.

2b
9pm

Mysterious ♩= c.108
S. 1
A. 1
CHOIR 1
T. 1
B. 1
pp
Ve-nus was the on - ly sail in a blue o - cean and the wood a
mp
When Ve-nus was the on - ly sail in
S. 2
A. 2
CHOIR 2
T. 2
B. 2
Sha - dow, sha - dow, sha - dow, sha - dow, sha - dow, sha - dow,

7
S. 1
doze of sha - dow, sha - dow, sha - dow, sha - dow, sha - dow,
A. 1
doze of sha - dow, sha - dow, sha - dow, sha - dow, sha - dow,
T. 1
a blue o - cean and the wood was a doze of sha -
B. 1
a blue o - cean and the wood was a doze of sha -
S. 2
sha - dow, Ve-nus was the on - ly sail in a blue o - cean and the wood a
A. 2
sha - dow, Ve-nus was the on - ly sail in a blue o - cean and the wood a
T. 2
mf
Wild-cat,
B. 2
mf
Wild-cat,

12
S. 1
sha - dow, crept to-wards me, crept to-wards me soft as fall - ing, fall-ing snow, as
A. 1
sha - dow, crept to-wards me, crept to-wards me soft as fall - ing, fall-ing snow, as
T. 1
mf
- dow, a sleek-ness crept to-wards me out of the trees
B. 1
mf
- dow, a sleek-ness crept to-wards me out of the trees
S. 2
doze of sha - dow, fall - ing, fall - ing, fall - ing, fall - ing,
A. 2
doze of sha - dow, fal - ling, fal - ling, fall - ing, fall - ing,
T. 2
Wild-cat, wild - cat.
B. 2
Wild-cat, wild - cat.

17
S. 1
soft as fall - ing, fall - ing, fall - ing, fall - ing,
A. 1
soft as fall - ing, fall - ing, fall - ing, fall - ing,
T. 1
mp
and soft as fall - ing snow a wild - cat
B. 1
mp
and soft as fall - ing snow a wild - cat
S. 2
fall - ing, crept to-wards me, crept to-wards me soft as fall - ing,
A. 2
fall - ing, crept to-wards me, crept to-wards me soft as fall - ing,
T. 2
Wild-cat,
B. 2
Wild-cat,

21
S. 1
fall - ing, fall - ing, fall - ing, fall - ing, fall - ing.
A. 1
fall - ing, fall - ing, fall - ing, fall - ing, fall - ing.
T. 1
came:
B. 1
came:
S. 2
fall - ing snow, as soft as fall - ing, fall - ing snow.
A. 2
fall - ing snow, as soft as fall - ing, fall - ing snow.
T. 2
Wild - cat, wild - cat.
B. 2
Wild - cat, wild - cat.
26
Slower ♩ = c.54
S. 1
p
Ah
A. 1
p
Ah
spoken unpitched and measured
S. 2
p
You have plan - ted a sharp dark - ness,
spoken unpitched and measured
A. 2
p
You have plan - ted a sharp dark - ness,
sing phrases independently and freely, entering at different times
T. 2
pp
dark - ness,
dark - ness,
sing phrases independently and freely, entering at different times
B. 2
pp
dark - ness,
dark - ness,

29
S. 1
A. 1
S. 2
A. 2
T. 2
B. 2
ah
ah
as if you were grow - ing a knife to cut your
as if you were grow - ing a knife to cut your
dark - ness, dark - ness,
dark - ness, dark - ness,
31
S. 1
A. 1
S. 2
A. 2
T. 2
B. 2
child - ren.
child - ren.
dark - - ness, dark - - ness,
dark - ness, dark - ness,

33
S. 1
A. 1
S. 2
A. 2
T. 2
B. 2
ah
ah
Wher-ev - er you tread the ground has grown sour,
Wher-ev - er you tread the ground has grown sour,
bit - ter wind, bit - ter, wind,
with your breath, with your breath,
35
S. 1
A. 1
S. 2
A. 2
T. 2
B. 2
ah
ah
the wind is bit - ter with your breath.
the wind is bit - ter with your breath.
bit - ter wind, bit - ter wind,
with your breath, with your breath,

37
A. 1
S. 2
A. 2
T. 2
B. 2
ah
When Man comes walk - ing ev' - ry - thing runs a -
When Man comes walk - ing ev' - ry - thing runs
runs a - way, runs a - way,
runs a - way, runs a - way,

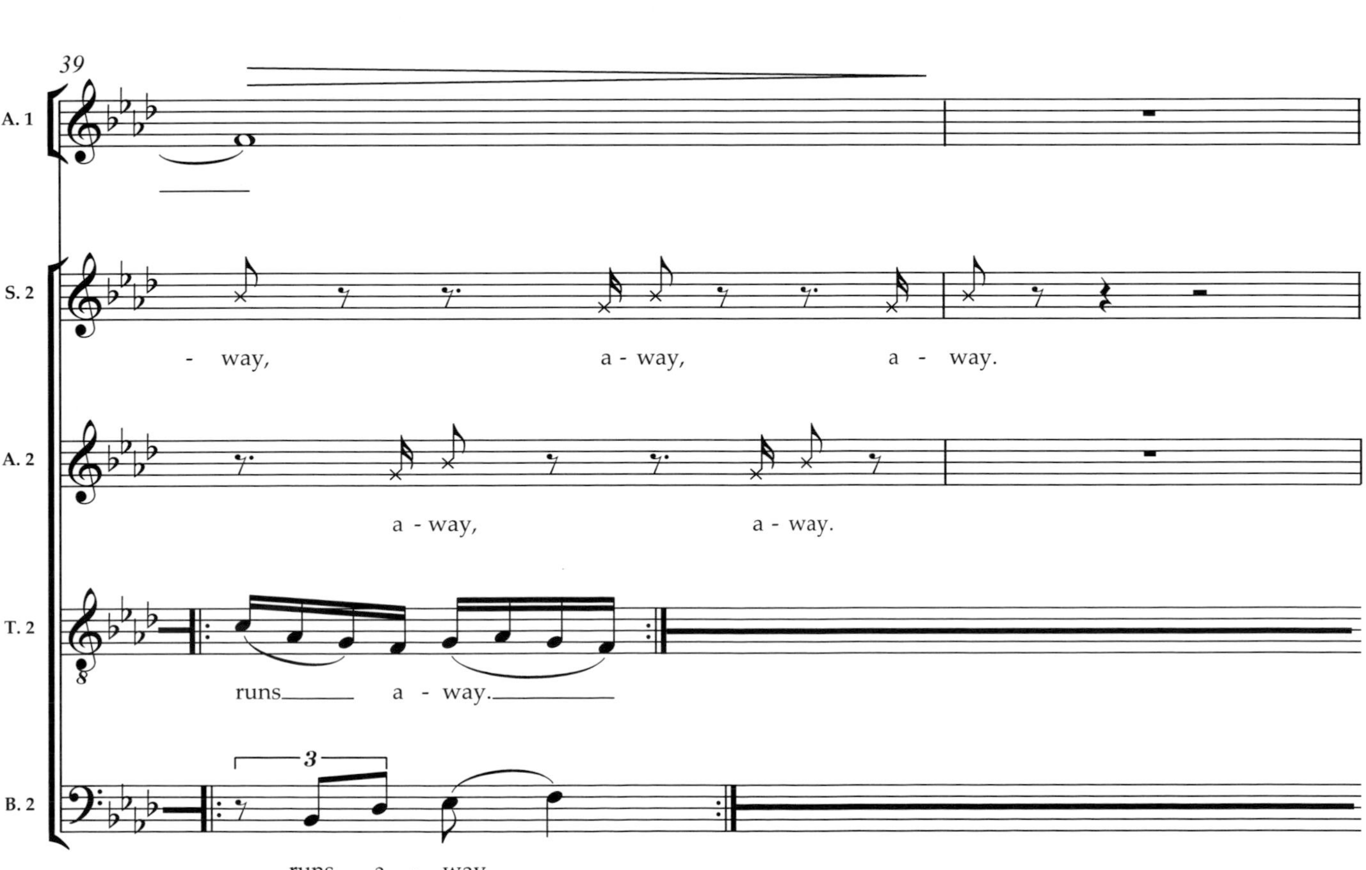
39
A. 1
S. 2
A. 2
T. 2
B. 2
- way, a - way, a - way.
a - way, a - way.
runs a - way.
runs a - way.

41
Tempo primo
pp
pp
mp
mp
pp
pp
mp
mp
S. 1
Dark tears, dark tears, dark tears, dark tears, dark tears,
A. 1
Dark tears, dark tears, dark tears, dark tears, dark tears,
T. 1
And the leaves of the
B. 1
And the leaves of the
S. 2
And the leaves of the trees were small
A. 2
And the leaves of the trees were small
T. 2
And the
B. 2
And the

47
S. 1
dark tears, dark tears, And the leaves of the trees were small dark tears,
A. 1
dark tears, dark tears, And the leaves of the trees were small dark tears,
T. 1
trees were small dark tears, And the leaves of the trees were dark
B. 1
trees were small dark tears, And the leaves of the trees were dark
S. 2
dark tears, dark tears, dark tears, dark tears, dark tears, dark tears,
A. 2
dark tears, dark tears, dark tears, dark tears, dark tears, dark tears,
T. 2
leaves of the trees were small dark tears, And the leaves of the
B. 2
leaves of the trees were small dark tears, And the leaves of the

53
S. 1
dark_ tears,___ dark tears, dark tears, dark tears, dark tears,
A. 1
dark_ tears,___ dark tears, dark tears, dark tears, dark tears,
T. 1
tears,___ as if the wood and all the woods of the Earth_
B. 1
tears,___ as if the wood and all the woods of the Earth_
S. 2
dark tears, if the wood and all the woods___ of the Earth,___ all the woods___
A. 2
dark tears, if the wood and all the woods___ of the Earth,___ all the woods___
T. 2
trees were dark tears,___ as if the wood and all the woods
B. 2
trees were dark tears,___ as if the wood and all the woods

58
S. 1
dark tears, if the wood and all the woods of the Earth, all the woods
A. 1
dark tears, if the wood and all the woods of the Earth, all the woods
T. 1
mp
were cry - ing them - selves to sleep, to sleep, to
B. 1
mp
were cry - ing them - selves to sleep, to sleep, to
S. 2
of the Earth, dark tears, dark tears, dark tears, dark tears,
A. 2
of the Earth, dark tears, dark tears, dark tears, dark tears,
T. 2
mp
of the Earth were cry - ing them - selves to sleep, to
B. 2
mp
of the Earth were cry - ing them - selves to sleep, to

63
S. 1
of the Earth, of the Earth.
A. 1
of the Earth, of the Earth.
T. 1
pp
sleep.
B. 1
pp
sleep.
S. 2
dark tears, dark tears, dark tears, dark tears, dark tears.
A. 2
dark tears, dark tears, dark tears, dark tears, dark tears.
T. 2
pp
sleep.
B. 2
pp
sleep.

2c

Green Rain

Playful and dance-like ♩. = *c*.84

CHILDREN'S CHOIR

CHOIR 1: S. 1, A. 1, T. 1, B. 1

mp

S. 1: Green rain, green rain, green rain, green

A. 1: Green rain, green rain, green rain, green rain,

T. 1: Green rain, green rain, green rain, green

B. 1: Green rain, green rain, green rain, green

8

mf

Children's Choir: By ditch-es and fal - len fen - ces we ga-ther to-ge-ther bid-ing our time un - til we have ta - ken

S. 1: rain, green rain, green rain, green

A. 1: green rain, green rain, green

T. 1: rain, green rain, green rain, green

B. 1: rain, green rain, green rain, green rain,

14

o - ver__ the whole field. We love what - ev - er's bro-ken or left be-hind. We

S. 1
rain,____ green____ rain,____ green________ rain, green,__

A. 1
rain, green____ rain,__ green________ rain, green,__

T. 1
rain, green rain, green________ rain, green,__

B. 1
________ green____ rain, green rain,______

19

mend the skin of earth where it's cut and hurt.________

S. 1
mf
green________ rain, green,__ green rain.____ Green rain,

A. 1
mf
green________ rain green,__ green rain.____ Green rain,____

T. 1
mf
green________ rain, green,__ green____ rain. Green rain,____
green rain.____ Green____ rain,________

B. 1
mf
green, rain,__________ green rain.____ Green_ rain,____ green

25
1.
f
By ditch - es and fal - len fen - ces we
2.
f
By ditch - es and fal - len fen - ces
S. 1
green rain, green rain,
A. 1
green rain, green rain,
T. 1
green rain, green rain,
green rain, green rain,
B. 1
rain, green rain, green
29
1.
ga - ther to - ge - ther bid - ing our time un - til we have ta - ken o - ver the
2.
we ga - ther to - ge - ther bid ing our time un - til we have ta - ken o -
S. 1
green rain, green rain,
A. 1
green rain, green rain,
T. 1
green rain, green rain,
green rain, green rain,
B. 1
rain, green rain, green

33
1.
whole field. We love what - ev - er's bro - ken or left be- hind. We
2.
- ver___ the whole field. We love what - ev - er's bro - ken or left be -
S. 1
green rain,___ green___ rain, green,__
A. 1
green___ rain, green___ rain, green,__
T. 1
green___ rain,___ green___ rain, green,__
green___
B. 1
__ rain,___ green__ rain,___
37
1.
mend the skin of earth where it's cut and hurt.___
2.
hind. We mend the skin of earth where it's cut and hurt.___
S. 1
green___ rain, green,___ green rain.___
A. 1
green___ rain green,___ green rain.___
T. 1
green___ rain, green,___ green___ rain.
B. 1
green__ rain,___ green rain.___

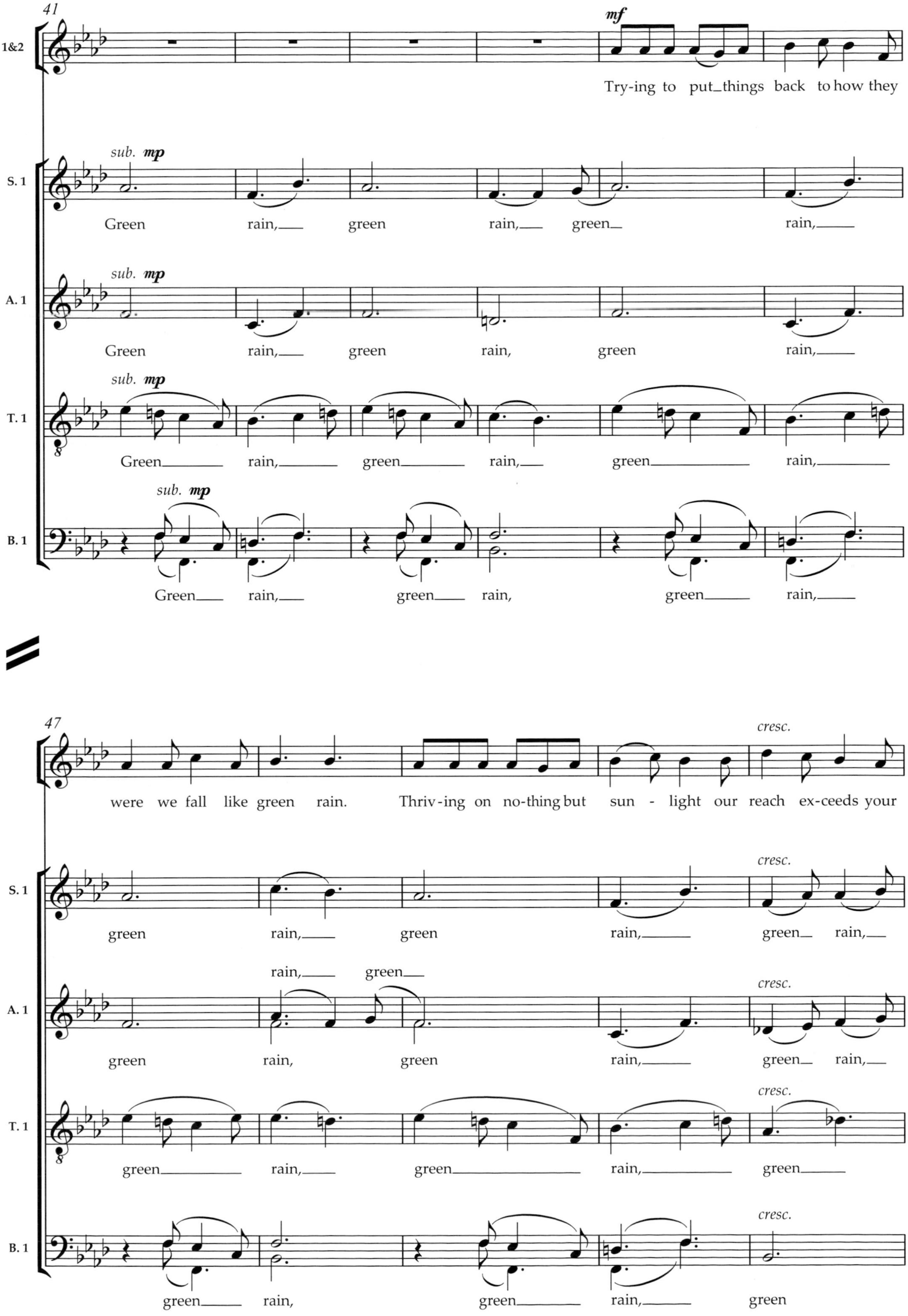
41
1&2
mf
Try-ing to put_things back to how they
S. 1
sub. mp
Green rain,___ green rain,___ green___ rain,___
A. 1
sub. mp
Green rain,___ green rain, green rain,___
T. 1
sub. mp
Green___ rain,___ green___ rain,___ green___ rain,___
B. 1
sub. mp
Green___ rain,___ green___ rain, green___ rain,___
47
were we fall like green rain. Thriv-ing on no-thing but sun - light our reach ex-ceeds your
cresc.
S. 1
green rain,___ green rain,___ green___ rain,___
cresc.
rain,___ green___
A. 1
green rain, green rain,___ green___ rain,___
cresc.
T. 1
green___ rain,___ green___ rain,___ green___
cresc.
B. 1
green___ rain, green___ rain,___ green
cresc.

52
grasp.
By ditch-es and fal - len
S. 1
green, green rain, green rain, green rain, green
A. 1
green rain, green rain, green rain, green
T. 1
rain, green rain, green rain, green
rain, green rain, green rain, green rain,
B. 1
rain, green rain, green rain, green
58
fen - ces we ga-ther to-ge-ther bid ing our time un - til we have ta - ken o - ver the
S. 1
rain, green rain, green rain,
A. 1
rain, green rain, green rain,
T. 1
rain, green rain, green rain,
green rain, green rain,
B. 1
rain, green rain, green rain, green
f

63

whole field. We love what - ev er's bro-ken or left be-hind. We mend the skin of earth where it's cut and

S. 1 green rain,___ green___ rain, green, green___ rain, green,_

A. 1 green_ rain, green___ rain, green, green___ rain, green,_

T. 1 green_ rain,___ green___ rain, green, green___ rain, green,_

B. 1 green_ ___ rain,___ green rain,___ green rain,___

69

hurt.___

S. 1 *sub.* **p** green rain.___ Green rain, green rain,___ green

A. 1 *sub.* **p** green rain.___ Green___ rain,___ green___ rain, green___

T. 1 *sub.* **p** green___ rain. Green___ rain,___ green___ rain,___ green___

B. 1 *sub.* **p** green rain.___ Green rain, green rain, green

76
p
Leave us a-lone, a - lone or else our kis-ses will give you goose - bumps.
S. 1
rain, green rain, green rain, green rain,
A. 1
rain, green rain, green rain, green rain,
T. 1
rain, green rain, green rain, green rain,
B. 1
rain, green rain, green rain, green rain,
83
pp
Leave us a-lone, a - lone or else our kis-ses will give you goose - bumps.
S. 1
green rain, green rain.
A. 1
green rain, green rain.
T. 1
green rain, green rain.
B. 1
green rain, green rain.

3a
Midnight

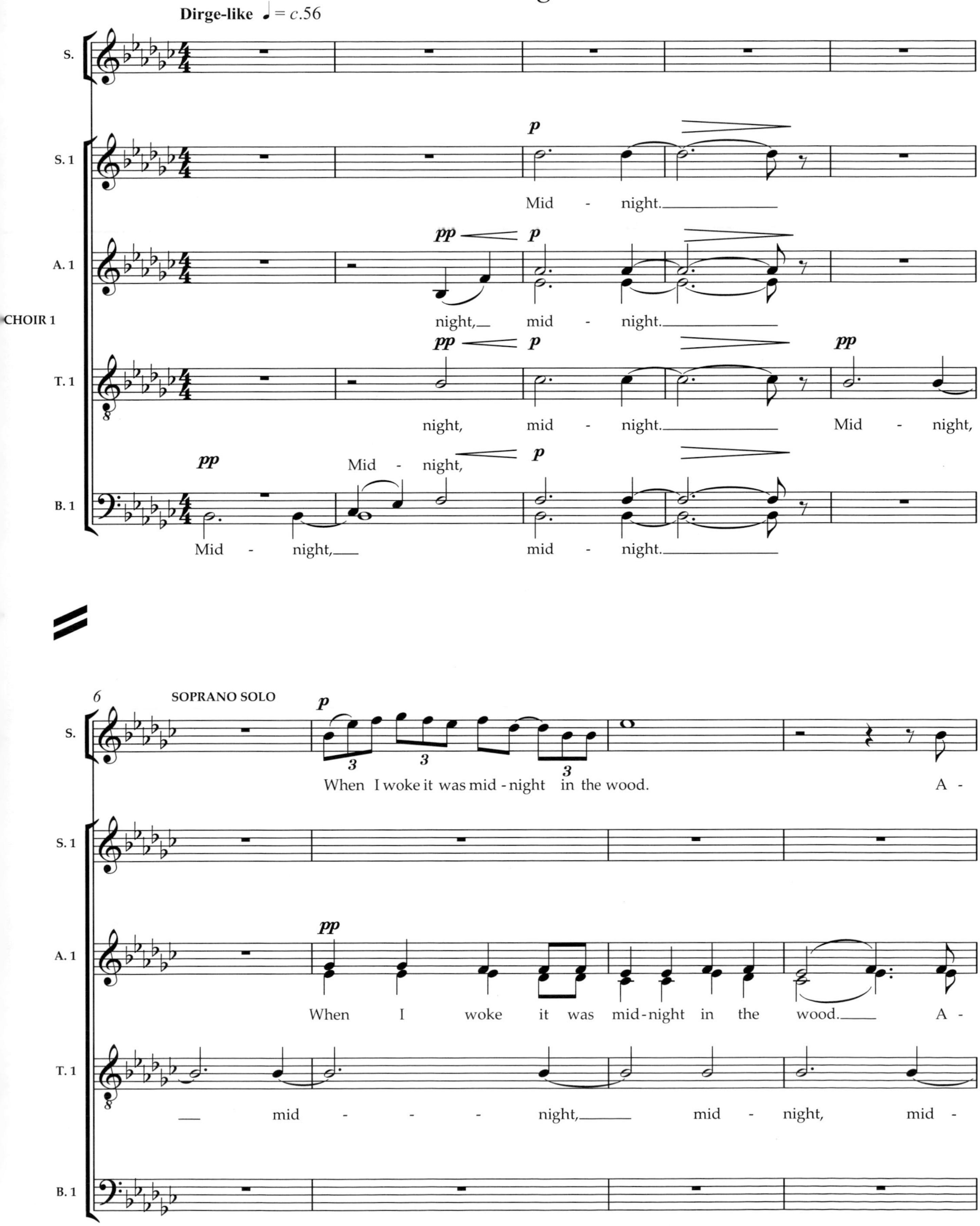

Dirge-like ♩ = *c*.56

S.
S. 1
A. 1
CHOIR 1
T. 1
B. 1

p Mid - night.
pp *p* night, mid - night.
pp *p* night, mid - night. *pp* Mid - night,
pp Mid - night, *p* Mid - night, mid - night.

10
S.
-bove_ my head a webbed stretch of dark - ness._
hung a high note, a
S. 1
hung a high note
A. 1
-bove my head a webbed stretch of dark - ness hung a high note
T. 1
- - night, mid - night, mid - night, mid - night,
B. 1
mid - night, mid - night, mid -
mp
p
pp
14
S.
high note_ on the edge of hear - ing._
At_ mid-night in the
S. 1
on the edge of hear - ing;_
A. 1
hear - ing;_ a
on the edge of hear - ing, hear - ing;_ horse - shoe bat, in
T. 1
mid - night, mid - night, mid - night._ Mid - - night,
B. 1
mid - night._
- night, mid - night, mid - night, mid - night.

19
S.
wood a horse - shoe bat, in tune to his own mu - sic:
S. 1
pp
mu - sic: I
A. 1
tune to his own mu - sic, own mu - sic, own mu - sic: I
T. 1
mu - sic, mu - sic, mu - sic:
B. 1
mu - - sic, mu - sic:
24
S. 1
hear the gla - cier break, the ice - cap creak be - neath a
A. 1
hear the gla - cier break, the ice - cap creak be - neath a
sing phrases independently and freely, entering at different times
B. 1
pp
mm
spoken unpitched and measured
S. 2
mp
gla-cier break, the ice-cap creak, creak be-
spoken unpitched and measured
A. 2
mp
gla-cier break, the ice-cap creak, creak be-
CHOIR 2
spoken unpitched and measured
T. 2
mf
I hear the gla-cier break, the ice-cap creak, creak be-neath a
spoken unpitched and measured
B. 2
mf
I hear the gla-cier break, the ice-cap creak, creak be-neath a

27
mp espress.
S.
Ah
S. 1
po - lar bear. I hear the thrum and
A. 1
po - lar bear. I hear the thrum and
B. 1
mm
S. 2
-neath a po - lar bear.
A. 2
-neath a po - lar bear.
Thrum and jud - der,
T. 2
po-lar bear.
I hear the thrum and jud-der,
B. 2
po-lar bear.
I hear the thrum and jud-der,

29
S.
ah
S. 1
jud - der, jud - der, whine and howl, the
A. 1
jud - der, jud - der, whine and howl, the
B. 1
S. 2
Thrum and jud-der, the whine and howl, the whole world
A. 2
the whine and howl, the whole world
T. 2
the whine and howl as the whole world
B. 2
the whine and howl as the whole world

31
mf
S.
ah
S. 1
p
whole world wails. You have smudged the light, have smudged the
A. 1
p
whole world wails. You have smudged the light, have smudged the
T. 1
spoken unpitched and measured
pp
mm
B. 1
mm
S. 2
mp
wails. The light,
A. 2
mp
wails. The light,
T. 2
mf
3
wails. You have smudged the light and made the
B. 2
mf
3
wails. You have smudged the light and made the

34
S.
mp
ah
S. 1
pp
light and made the dark - ness pale: be si - lent, si - lent
A. 1
pp
light and made the dark - ness pale: be si - lent, si - lent
B. 1
mm
S. 2
dark-ness pale: si - lent now
A. 2
dark-ness pale: si - lent now
T. 2
dark-ness pale: be si - lent now
B. 2
dark-ness pale: be si - lent now

37
S.
S. 1
now and learn to lis - ten, lis - ten to the Earth.
A. 1
now and learn to lis - ten, lis - ten to the Earth.
B. 1
mm
S. 2
p
to lis-ten to the Earth, to the
A. 2
p
to lis-ten to the Earth, to the
T. 2
mp
and learn how to lis-ten to the Earth, to the Earth.
B. 2
mp
and learn how to lis-ten to the Earth, to the Earth.

40
S.
S. 1
p
Mid - night.
A. 1
pp p
- night, mid - night.
T. 1
pp p pp
- night, mid - night. Mid - night,
Mid - night,
B. 1
pp p
Mid - night, mid - night.
S. 2
Earth.
A. 2
Earth.
46
S.
p
3
By then the moon was o - pen. And all a - round me corp-ses
S. 1
p
All a - round me corp-ses
A. 1
pp p
Then, by then the moon, the moon was o - pen. All a - round me corp-ses
T. 1
p
mid - - night, mid - night. All a - round me corp-ses
B. 1
p
All a -

51
S.
came from curb - sides, all a - round me.
S. 1
came from curb - sides, came to nests and bur - rows they'd left be -
A. 1
came from curb - sides, came to nests and bur - rows they'd left be -
T. 1
came from curb - sides, came to nests and bur - rows they'd left be -
B. 1
-round me, to bur - rows they'd left be -
54
S.
S. 1
- hind.
A. 1
- hind, lay down, and fell a - sleep for the last time.
T. 1
- hind, down, fell a - sleep for the last time.
down, fell a - sleep for the last time.
pp
B. 1
- hind, down, a - sleep the last time. Mid - night,

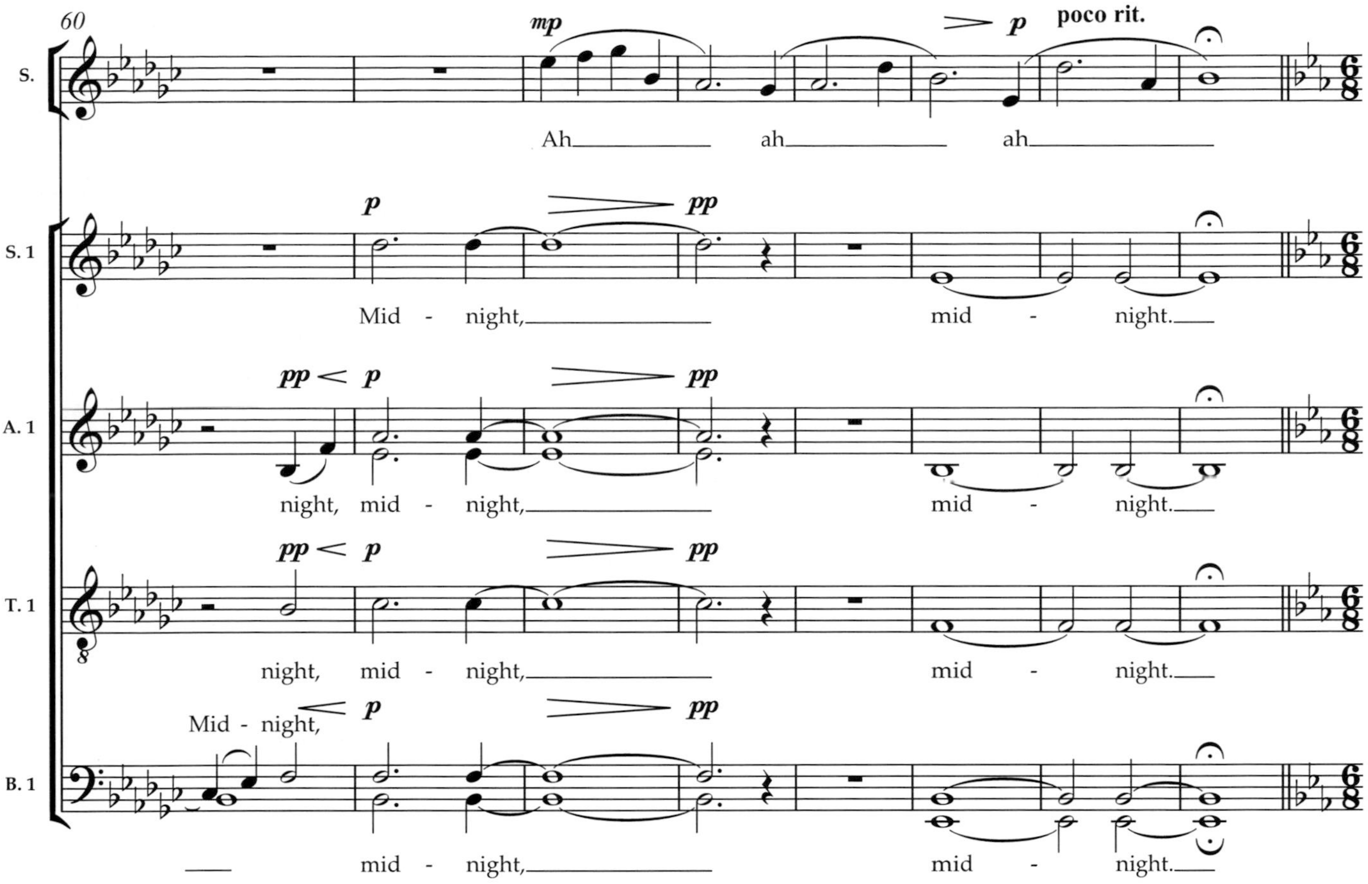

60

poco rit.

S. — *mp* Ah ah ah *p*

S. 1 — *p* Mid - night, *pp* mid - night.

A. 1 — *pp* *p* night, mid - night, *pp* mid - night.

T. 1 — *pp* *p* night, mid - night, *pp* mid - night.

B. 1 — Mid - night, *p* mid - night, *pp* mid - night.

3b

We need

6
S.
A.
T.
B.
ff
Give me a hand and we'll put it to sleep, we'll put it to sleep, put it to sleep for - ev - er, put it to
Give me a hand and we'll put it to sleep, we'll put it to sleep, put it to sleep for - ev - er, put it to
hand, we'll put it to sleep, put it to sleep, put it to sleep, to sleep for - ev - er,
hand, we'll put it to sleep, put it to sleep, put it to sleep, to sleep for - ev - er,
11
con forza
sleep_ for - ev - er. Chain - saws whine and howl as the fo - rest dies, the fo - rest
sleep_ for - ev - er. Chain - saws whine and howl as the fo - rest dies, the fo - rest
sleep_ for - ev - er. Chain - saws whine and howl as the fo - rest dies, the fo - rest dies, the
sleep_ for - ev - er. Chain - saws whine and howl as the fo - rest dies, the fo - rest dies, the
16
f
dies, the fo - rest dies: it's all in a day's work. What good is a fo - rest
dies, the fo - rest dies: it's all in a day's work. What good is a fo - rest
fo - rest, fo - rest dies: it's all in a day's work. What good is a fo - rest a - ny-
fo - rest, fo - rest dies: it's all in a day's work. What good is a fo - rest fo - rest a - ny-

21
ff
S.
a - ny-way, a fo - rest a - ny - way? We need more land, we
A.
a - ny-way, a fo - rest a - ny - way? We need more food, we need more land, we
T.
-way, a - ny, a - ny-way? We need more land, we need more food, we need more land, we
B.
-way, a - ny, a - ny-way? We need more land, we need more food, we need more land, we

26
fff
S.
need more food, we need more land, we need more food, we need, we need, we need.
A.
need more food, we need more land, we need more food, we need, we need, we need.
T.
need more food, we need, we need_more land, we need_more food, we need, we need.
B.
need more food, we need, we need_more land, we need_more food, we need, we need.

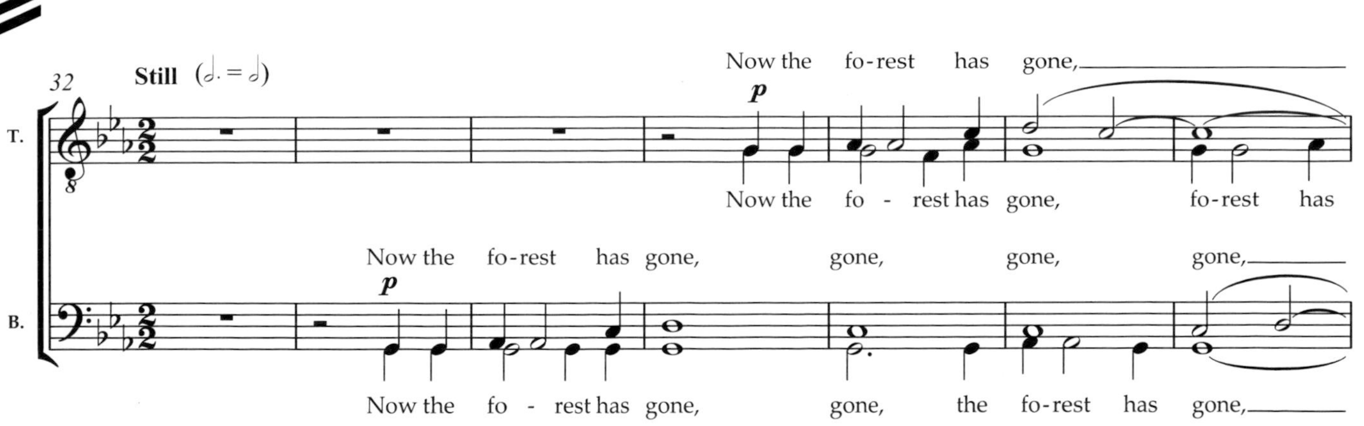
32
Still (𝅗𝅥. = 𝅗𝅥)
p
T.
Now the fo-rest has gone,
Now the fo - rest has gone, fo-rest has
B.
Now the fo-rest has gone, gone, gone, gone,
Now the fo - rest has gone, gone, the fo-rest has gone,

39
S.
A.
T.
B.
p
mp dolce
how qui - et it is! How qui - et it is!
how qui - et it is! How qui - et it is!
gone, qui - et it is! How qui - et it is!
fo - rest has
— qui - et it is! How qui - et it is! Now the fo - rest has

46
S.
A.
T.
B.
poco rit.
p
pp
has gone, gone.
has gone, gone.
Now the fo - rest has gone,
Now the fo - rest has gone, gone, gone.
gone, gone, gone,
gone, gone, the fo - rest has gone, gone.

3c
3am

Expressive but with a sense of ritual ♩ = c.80

6

A. 1
mm

T. 1
p
I woke at three to the creak - ing call of the corn -

B. 1
p
Woke at three, corn -

A. 2
-em ae - ter - nam, (*mm*)

T. 2
p
I woke at three to the creak - ing call of the corn -

B. 2
p
I woke at three to the creak - ing call of the corn -

14

A. 1
mm

T. 1
- crake, a croak or click from the throat of

B. 1
- crake, croak from the throat of

A. 2
re - qui - em ae - ter - nam, (*mm*)

T. 2
- crake, a croak or click from the throat of

B. 2
- crake, a croak or click from the throat of

21
S. 1
mp
I am bro-ken and hoarse from re - cit ing a re-gis-ter of the
A. 1
mp
I am bro-ken, hoarse from re - cit ing re-gis-ter of the
T. 1
"Crex crex:"
B. 1
"Crex crex:"
S. 2
mp
bro-ken and hoarse from re - cit ing a re-gis-ter of the
A. 2
mp
Re - qui - em ae - ter - nam, (mm) bro - ken, bro - ken of the
T. 2
"Crex crex:"
B. 2
"Crex crex:"
30
S. 1
dead, of those who can no long - er speak for them-
A. 1
dead, of those who can no long - er speak for them-
T. 1
mp
re - qui - em ae - ter - nam, (mm)
S. 2
dead, of those who can no long - er speak for them-
A. 2
dead, of those who no long - er speak for them-
T. 2
mp
mm

38
S. 1
- selves.
Re - qui - em,
re - qui-
A. 1
- selves.
Re - qui - em,
re - qui-
T. 1
re - qui - em ae - ter - nam, (mm)
B. 1
The Heath Hen and Bush-wren,
S. 2
- selves.
Re - qui - em,
re - qui-
A. 2
- selves.
Re - qui - em,
re - qui-
B. 2
The Heath Hen and Bush-wren,
45
S. 1
-em ae - ter - nam,
A. 1
-em ae - ter - nam,
T. 1
re - qui - em ae - ter - nam,
B. 1
the Bar-ba-ry Lion, the Laugh-ing Owl and Gol-den Toad,
S. 2
-em ae - ter - nam,
A. 2
-em ae - ter - nam,
B. 2
the Bar-ba-ry Lion, the Laugh-ing Owl and Gol-den Toad,

50
S. 1
re - qui - em ae - ter - nam.
A. 1
re - qui - em ae - ter - nam.
T. 1
(mm)
re - qui - em ae - ter - nam,
B. 1
the Ba - li Ti - ger, Cas - pian Ti - ger, Ja - van Ti - ger,
S. 2
re - qui - em ae - ter - nam.
A. 2
re - qui - em ae - ter - nam.
T. 2
p
mm
B. 2
the Ba - li Ti - ger, Cas - pian Ti - ger, Ja - van Ti - ger,

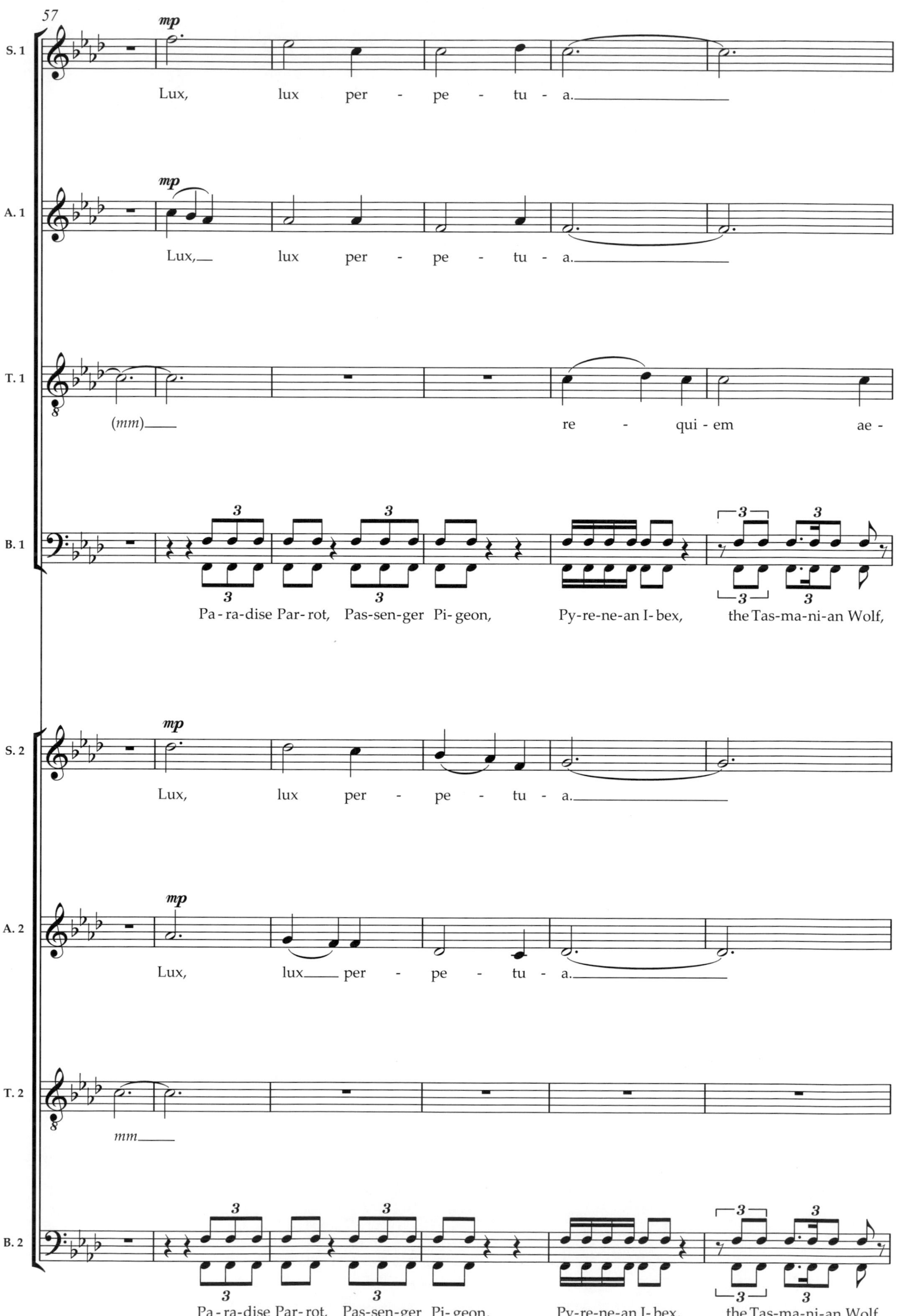
57
S. 1
mp
Lux, lux per - pe - tu - a.
A. 1
mp
Lux, lux per - pe - tu - a.
T. 1
(mm)
re - qui - em ae -
B. 1
Pa - ra - dise Par - rot, Pas - sen - ger Pi - geon, Py - re - ne - an I - bex, the Tas - ma - ni - an Wolf,
S. 2
mp
Lux, lux per - pe - tu - a.
A. 2
mp
Lux, lux per - pe - tu - a.
T. 2
mm
B. 2
Pa - ra - dise Par - rot, Pas - sen - ger Pi - geon, Py - re - ne - an I - bex, the Tas - ma - ni - an Wolf,

63
S. 1
Re - qui - em ae - ter - nam,
A. 1
Re - qui - em ae - ter - nam,
T. 1
- ter - nam, (mm)
B. 1
Wake Is-land Rail, Thick-tail Chub,
S. 2
Re - qui - em ae - ter - nam,
A. 2
Re - qui - em ae - ter - nam,
T. 2
mm
re - qui -
B. 2
Wake Is-land Rail, Thick-tail Chub,

69
S. 1
re - - qui - em ae - ter - - nam, ae -
A. 1
re - - qui - em ae - ter - - nam, ae -
T. 1
B. 1
the Pa-les-ti-nian Paint ed Frog, the West-ern Black Rhi - no - ce- ros......
S. 2
re - - qui - em ae - ter - - nam, ae -
A. 2
re - - qui - em ae - ter - - nam, ae -
T. 2
- em.
B. 2
the Pa-les-ti-nian Paint ed Frog, the West-ern Black Rhi - no - ce - ros......

73
p
mp espress.
f
S. 1
-ter - nam.
He called all night and their
A. 1
-ter - nam.
He called all night and their
T. 1
He called all night and their
B. 1
He called all night, their
S. 2
-ter - nam.
A. 2
-ter - nam.
T. 2
re - qui - em ae - ter - nam. (mm)
B. 2

80
S. 1
names were nu - me - rous as stars. Re - qui - em ae - ter - nam. Sem-
A. 1
names were nu - me - rous as stars. Re - qui - em ae - ter - nam. Sem - pi -
T. 1
names were nu - me - rous as stars. Re - qui - em ae - ter - nam. Sem-pi -
B. 1
names were nu - mer - rous as stars. Re - qui - em, re - qui - em ae -
S. 2
mf cresc.
f
ff
Re - qui - em, re - qui - em ae - ter - nam.
A. 2
Re - qui - em, re - qui - em ae - ter - nam.
T. 2
Re - qui - em, re - qui - em ae - ter - nam.
B. 2
Re - qui - em, re - qui - em ae - ter - nam.

88
S. 1
- pi - ter - nam re - qui - em. Sem - pi - ter - nam re - qui - em.
A. 1
-ter - nam re - qui - em, re - qui - em. Sem-pi - ter - nam re - qui - em.
T. 1
-ter - nam re - qui - em. Sem - pi - ter - nam re - qui - em.
B. 1
-ter - nam, re - qui - em. Sem - pi - ter - nam re - qui - em.
S. 2
Sem - pi - ter-nam re - qui - em. Sem-pi - ter - nam re - qui - em.
A. 2
Sem - pi - ter-nam re - qui - em. Sem-pi - ter - nam re - qui - em.
T. 2
Sem - pi - ter-nam re - qui - em. Sem-pi - ter - nam re - qui - em.
B. 2
Sem - pi - ter - nam re - qui - em. Sem-pi - ter - nam re - qui - em.

96
S. 1
f dim.
mp
Re - qui - em ae - ter - nam, ae - ter - - nam.
A. 1
f dim.
mp
Re - qui - em ae - ter - nam, ae - ter - - nam.
T. 1
f dim.
mp
Re - qui - em ae - ter - nam, ae - ter - nam, re - qui -
B. 1
f dim.
mp
Re - qui - em, re - qui - em ae - ter - - nam, ae -
S. 2
f dim.
mp
Re - qui - em ae - ter - nam, ae - ter - - nam.
A. 2
f dim.
mp
Re - qui - em ae - ter - nam, ae - ter - - nam.
T. 2
f dim.
mp
Re - qui - em ae - ter - nam, ae - ter - nam, ae - ter - nam,
B. 2
f dim.
mp
Re - qui - em, re - qui - em ae - ter - - nam, ae -

104
S. 1
A. 1
p
Re - qui - em ae - ter - nam, (mm) re - qui - em ae -
T. 1
- em.
B. 1
p
- ter - - - nam.
S. 2
A. 2
p
mm
T. 2
p
re - qui - em.
B. 2
p
- ter - - - nam.

112
A. 1
-ter - nam, (mm)
T. 1
p
He called all night and their names were nu - me - rous as
B. 1
p
called all night, as
A. 2
mm
T. 2
p
He called all night and their names were nu - me - rous as
B. 2
p
He called all night and their names were nu - me - rous as
119
S. 1
p
Lux per - pe - tu - a,
A. 1
re - qui - em ae - ter - nam, (mm)
T. 1
stars, their names were nu - me - rous as
B. 1
stars, names nu - me - rous as
S. 2
p
Lux per - pe - tu - a,
A. 2
Lux per - pe - tu - a,
T. 2
stars, Their names were nu - me - rous as
B. 2
stars, their names were nu - me - rous as

126
S. 1
Lux per - pe - tu - a,
re - qui - em ae -
A. 1
re - qui - em ae - ter - nam, (mm)
re - qui - em ae -
T. 1
stars,
as stars,
as
B. 1
stars,
as stars,
as
S. 2
Lux per - pe - tu - a,
re - qui - em ae -
A. 2
Lux per - pe - tu - a,
re - qui -
T. 2
stars,
as stars,
as
B. 2
stars,
as stars,
as

132
S. 1
A. 1
T. 1
B. 1
S. 2
A. 2
T. 2
B. 2
pp
- ter - nam.
- ter - nam, re - qui - em ae - ter - nam,
stars, stars.
- ter - - nam.
-em ae - ter - - nam.

137
rit.
S. 1
A. 1
(mm)
re - qui - em ae - ter - nam, (mm)
T. 1
B. 1
S. 2
A. 2
pp
mm
mm
T. 2
B. 2

3d
Sorry too late

7
S.
A.
T.
B.
We have
We have
We have
We have
S. 1
A. 1
T. 1
B. 1
ff
The flo - wers, the flo-wers are felled, the flo-wers are felled un - der con - crete.
flo - wers are felled, the flo-wers are felled, the flo-wers are felled un - der con - crete.
felled, are felled, are felled, flo-wers are felled, are felled un - der con - crete.
flo - wers, the flo - wers are felled, flo-wers are felled, are felled un - der con - crete.
S. 2
A. 2
T. 2
B. 2
ff
The flo - wers are felled un - der con - crete.
ff
The flo - wers are felled un - der con - crete.
ff
The flo - wers are felled un - der con - crete.
ff
The flo - wers are felled un - der con - crete.

11
S.
done those things we ought not to have done.
A.
done those things we ought not to have done.
T.
done those things we ought not to have done.
B.
done those things we ought not to have done.
S. 1
The o - cean is
A. 1
The o - cean is smirched, is
T. 1
The o-cean is smirched with oil, with
B. 1
The o-cean is smirched with oil, is smirched with
S. 2
The
A. 2
The
T. 2
The
B. 2
The

16
S. 1
smirched with oil, is smirched with oil, smirched with oil, with
A. 1
smirched with oil, is smirched with oil, smirched with oil,___ with
T. 1
oil, smirched with oil, smirched with oil, is smirched with
B. 1
oil, smirched with oil, smirched with oil, is smirched with
S. 2
o - cean, the o - cean is smirched___ with
A. 2
o - cean, the o - cean is smirched___ with
T. 2
o - cean, the o - cean is smirched___ with
B. 2
o - cean, the o - cean is smirched___ with

19
S.
We have left un - done those things we
A.
We have left un - done those things we
T.
We have left un - done those things we
B.
We have left un - done those things we
S. 1
oil, the o-cean is smirched with oil.
A. 1
oil, the o-cean is smirched with oil.
T. 1
oil, smirched with oil.
B. 1
oil, smirched with oil.
S. 2
oil, is smirched with oil.
A. 2
oil, is smirched with oil.
T. 2
oil, is smirched with oil.
B. 2
oil, is smirched with oil.

25
S.
ought to have done.
A.
ought to have done.
T.
ought to have done.
B.
ought to have done.
S. 1
Mo-tor-ways thrum and jud - der, thrum and jud - der, thrum and
A. 1
Mo-tor-ways thrum and jud - der, thrum and jud - der, thrum and
T. 1
Mo-tor-ways thrum and jud - der, thrum and jud - der, thrum and jud - der,
B. 1
Mo-tor-ways thrum and jud - der, thrum and jud - der, thrum and jud - der,
S. 2
thrum and jud - der,
A. 2
thrum and jud - der,
T. 2
thrum and jud - der,
B. 2
thrum and jud - der,

29
S.
And there is no health in
A.
And there is no health in
T.
And there is no health in
B.
And there is no health in
S. 1
jud - der, thrum and jud - der, thrum and jud - der.
A. 1
jud - der,thrum and jud - der, thrum and jud - der.
T. 1
jud - der,thrum and jud - der, thrum and jud - der.
B. 1
jud - der,thrum and jud - der, thrum and jud - der. We are
S. 2
thrum and jud - der, jud - der, thrum and jud - der.
A. 2
thrum and jud - der, jud - der, thrum and jud - der.
T. 2
thrum and jud - der, jud - der, thrum and jud - der.
B. 2
thrum and jud - der, jud - der, thrum and jud - der.

34
S.
us.
We are sor-ry too late, too late,
A.
us.
We are sor-ry too late, too late,
T.
us.
We are sor-ry too late, too late,
B.
us.
We are sor-ry too late, too late,
S. 1
We are sor-ry too late, are sor-ry too late, sor-ry too late as al - ways.
A. 1
We are sor-ry too late, are sor-ry too late, sor-ry too late as al - ways. the
T. 1
We are sor-ry too late, are sor-ry too late, sor-ry too late, too late. The whole world wails, the
B. 1
sor-ry too late as al - ways, sor-ry too late, sor-ry too late, too late. The whole world wails, the
S. 2
We are sor-ry too late, we are sor-ry too late, too
A. 2
We are sor-ry too late, we are sor-ry too late, too
T. 2
We are sor-ry too late, we are sor-ry too late, too
B. 2
We are sor-ry too late, we are sor-ry too late, too

39
S.
too late, are sor - ry too late, are sor - ry too late, are sor - ry too late, we are
A.
too late, are sor - ry too late, are sor - ry too late, are sor - ry too late, we are
T.
too late, are sor - ry too late, are sor - ry too late, are sor - ry too late, we are
B.
too late, are sor - ry too late, are sor - ry too late, are sor - ry too late, we are
S. 1
The whole world wails, the whole world wails. We are sor - ry too late, are
A. 1
whole world wails, the whole world wails, the whole world wails. We are sor - ry too late, are
T. 1
whole world wails, the whole world wails, the whole world wails. Too late, are sor - ry too
B. 1
whole world wails, the whole world wails, the whole world wails. Too late, are sor - ry too
S. 2
late, too late, are sor - ry too late are sor - ry too late, are sor - ry too
A. 2
late, too late, are sor - ry too late are sor - ry too late, are sor - ry too
T. 2
late, too late, are sor - ry too late are sor - ry too late, are sor - ry too
B. 2
late, too late, are sor - ry too late are sor - ry too late, are sor - ry too

43
S.
sor - ry too late, are sor - ry too late as al - ways.
A.
sor - ry too late, are sor - ry too late as al - ways.
T.
sor - ry too late, are sor - ry too late as al - ways.
B.
sor - ry too late, are sor - ry too late as al - ways.
S. 1
sor - ry too late, are sor - ry too late, are sor - ry too late as al - ways.
A. 1
sor - ry too late, are sor - ry too late, are sor - ry too late as al - ways.
T. 1
late, are sor - ry too late, are sor - ry too late, are sor - ry as al - ways.
B. 1
late, are sor - ry too late, are sor - ry too late, are sor - ry as al - ways.
S. 2
late, we are sor - ry too late as al - ways.
A. 2
late, we are sor - ry too late as al - ways.
T. 2
late, we are sor - ry too late as al - ways.
B. 2
late, we are sor - ry too late as al - ways.
fff

4a
Peppermint freckles

Folksy and light ♩. = *c*.84

CHILDREN'S CHOIR *mf*
We're

CHAMBER CHOIR

S. *mp*
La la la la la la la la la la la la la la la la

A. *mp*
La la la la la la la la la

T. *mp*
La___ la la la la___ la la la la la_

B. *mp*
La___ la___ la___ la___

9

CHIL. CHOIR
print-ing the form of our fa - ces on the mea-dow,___ smel-ling of fresh___ air and clear_

S.
la la la la la la la la la la la la la la la
la la la la la

A.
la la la la la la la la la la la

T.
_ la___ la la la la__ la la

B.
la___ la___ la___ la_

15
1.
skies. Pep-per-mint freck-les, pep-per-mint freck-les, pep-per-mint, pep-per-mint
2.
skies. Pep-per-mint freck-les, pep-per-mint freck-les, pep-per-mint,
S.
la la la la la la la la la
A.
la la la la la la la la la
T.
la la la la la la
B.
la la la la
20
1.
freck-les, pep-per-mint freck-les, pep-per-mint freck-les, pep-per-mint, pep-per-mint
2.
pep-per-mint freck-les, pep-per-mint freck-les, pep-per-mint freck-les, pep-per-mint
S.
la pep-per-mint freck-les, la la oh pep-per-mint freck-les, la
A.
la la la la la la
T.
la la oh pep-per-mint freck-les, la
B.
la la la la la

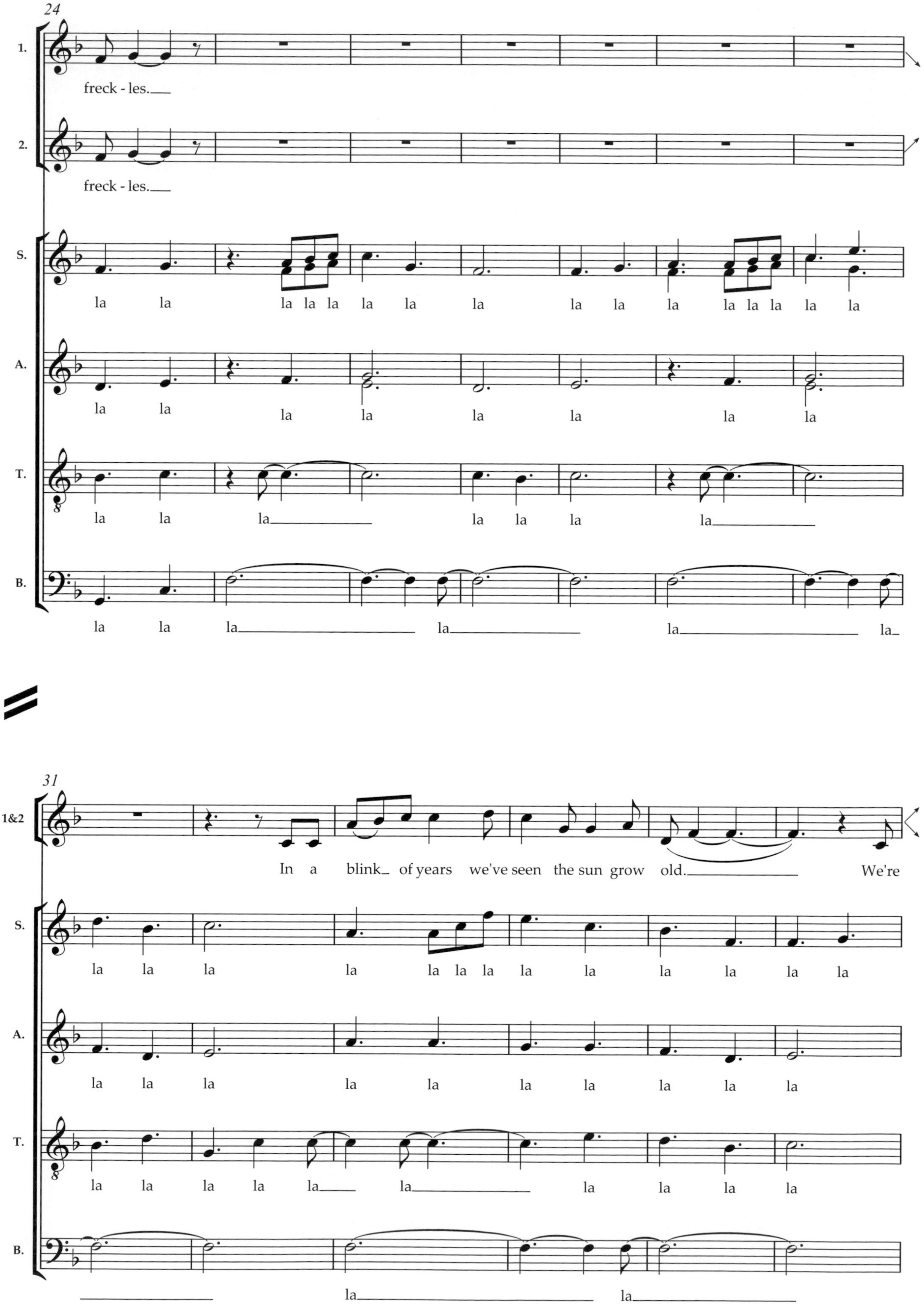
24
1.
freck - les.
2.
freck - les.
S.
la la la la la la la la la la la la la la la la
A.
la la la la la la la la
T.
la la la la la la la
B.
la la la la la la
31
1&2
In a blink of years we've seen the sun grow old. We're
S.
la la la la la la la la la la la la la
A.
la la la la la la la la la la
T.
la la la la la la la la la la la
B.
la la

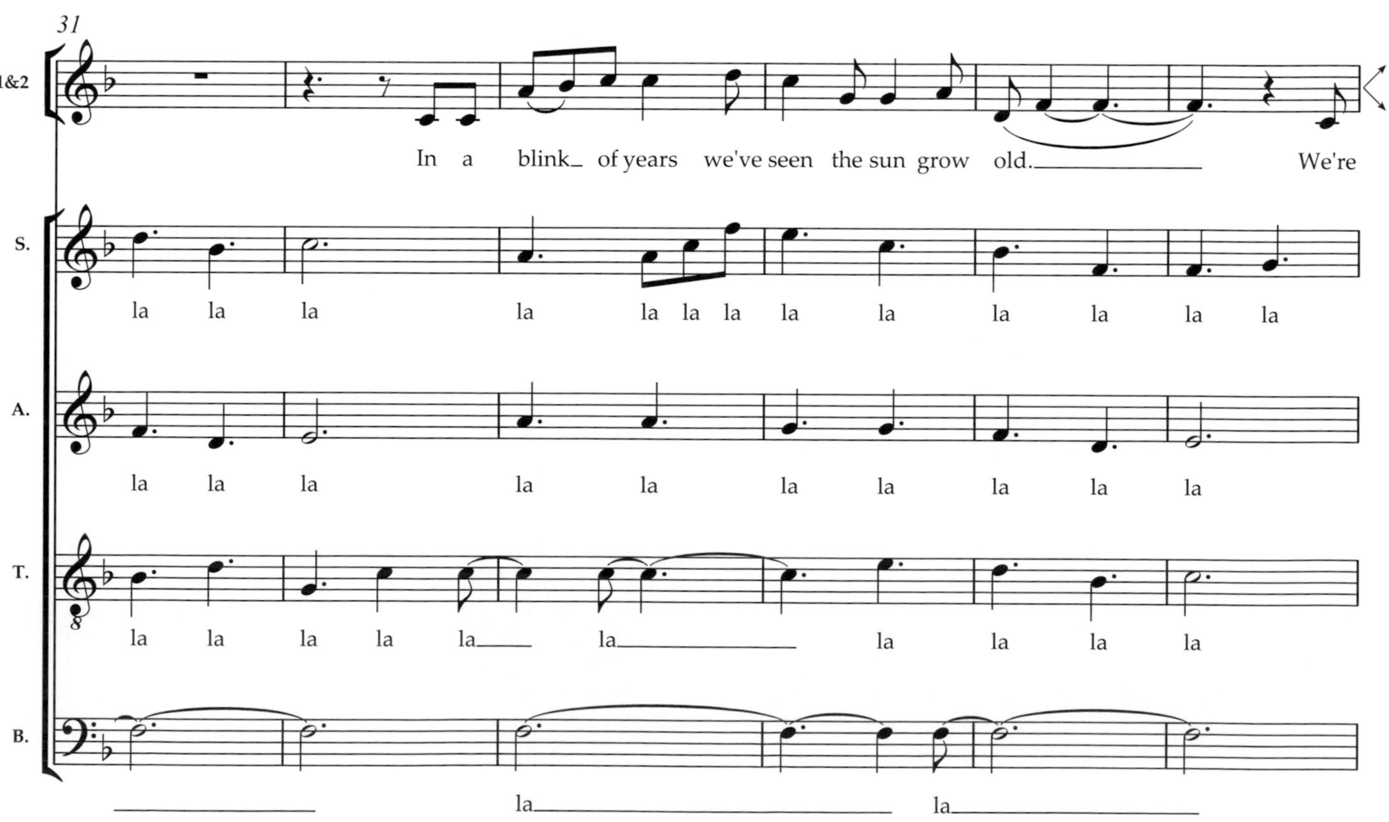

37
1.
neat and un - ti - dy and like to re - peat our - selves.
2.
neat and un - ti - dy and like to re - peat our - selves.
S.
la la la la la la la la la la
A.
la la la la la la la la la la
T.
la la la la la la
B.
la la la
41
1.
Pep-per-mint freck-les, pep - per-mint freck-les, pep - per- mint, pep-per - mint freck - les,
2.
Pep - per-mint freck-les, pep - per-mint freck-les, pep-per- mint, pep - per-mint freck-les,
S.
la la la la la la pep - per- mint
A.
la la la la la la la
T.
la la la la la
B.
la la la la la

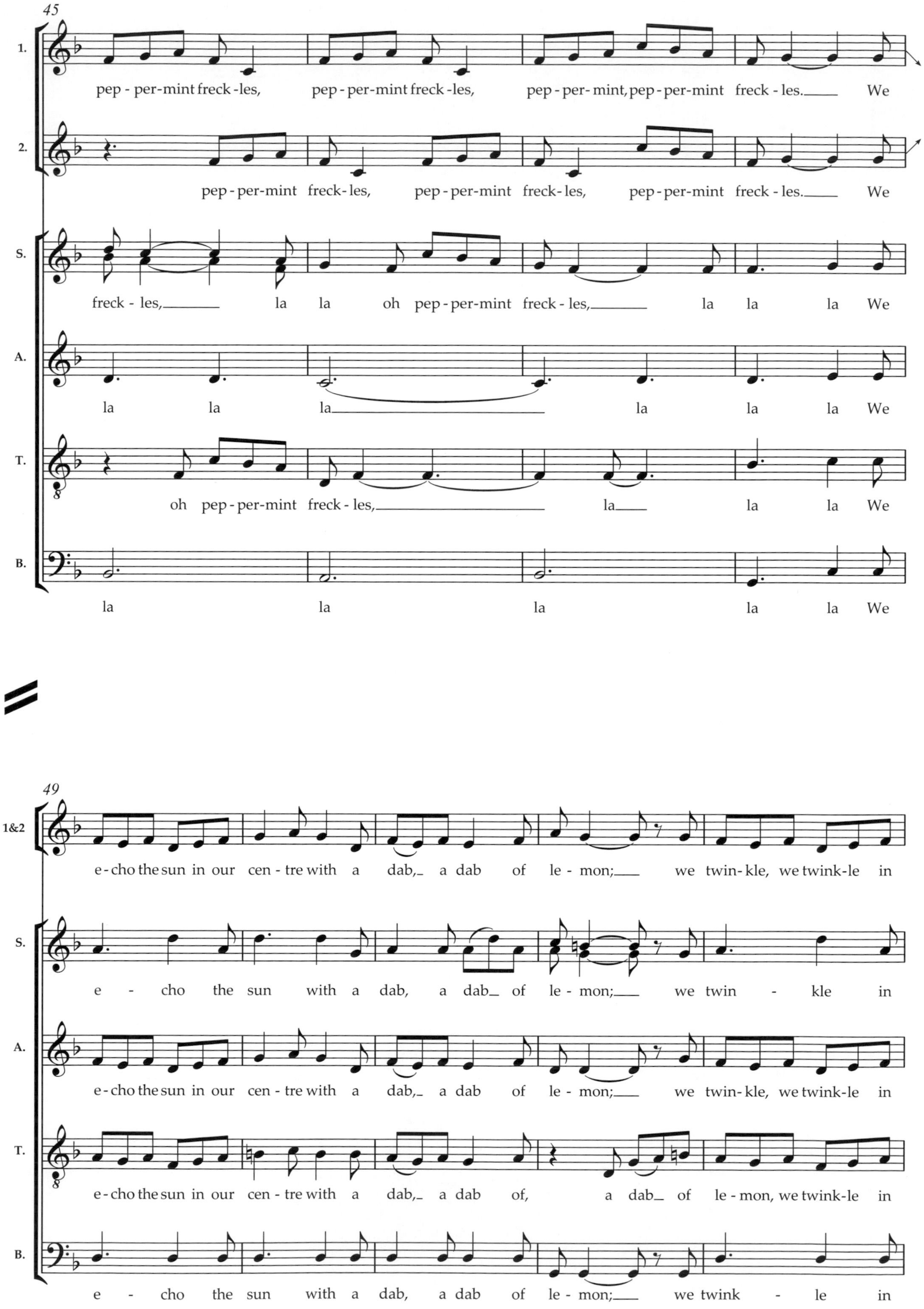

45

1. pep - per-mint freck -les, pep - per-mint freck -les, pep - per- mint, pep - per-mint freck - les. We

2. pep - per-mint freck-les, pep - per-mint freck-les, pep - per-mint freck - les. We

S. freck - les, la la oh pep - per-mint freck - les, la la la We

A. la la la la la la We

T. oh pep - per-mint freck - les, la la la We

B. la la la la la We

54
1&2
S.
A.
T.
B.
sprink-led con-stel - la - tions.
sprink-led con-stel - la - tions. La la la la la la la la
sprink-led con-stel la - tions. La la la la
sprink-led con-stel - la - tions. La la la la
sprink-led con-stel - la - tions. La la

61
1&2
S.
A.
T.
B.
You all look the same to us.
la la la la la la la la la la la la la la la la la
la la la la la la la la la la la
la la la la la la la la la la
la la la la

73

1st TIME: *mf*
2nd TIME: *f*

1.
Pep-per-mint freck- les, pep - per-mint freck- les, pep - per- mint, pep-per - mint freck les,

2.
Pep - per-mint freck- les, pep - per-mint freck- les, pep-per- mint, pep - per-mint freck- les,

1st TIME: *mf*
2nd TIME: *f*

S.
la la la la la la pep - per- mint

1st TIME: *mf*
2nd TIME: *f*

A.
la la
la la la la la

1st TIME: *mf*
2nd TIME: *f*

T.
la la la la la

1st TIME: *mf*
2nd TIME: *f*

B.
la la la la la

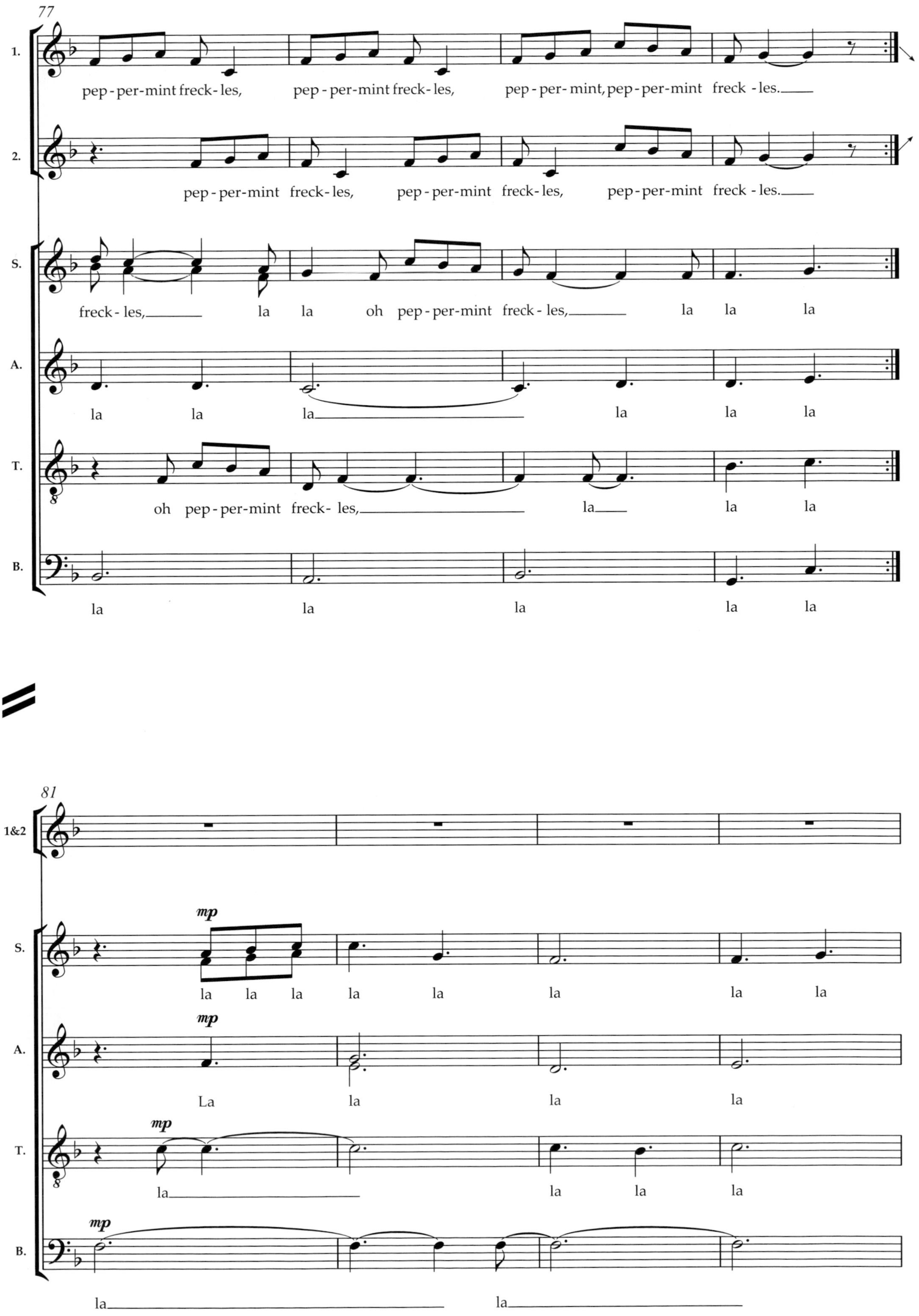

77

1. pep - per - mint freck - les, pep - per - mint freck - les, pep - per - mint, pep - per - mint freck - les.

2. pep - per - mint freck - les, pep - per - mint freck - les, pep - per - mint freck - les.

S. freck - les, la la oh pep - per - mint freck - les, la la la

A. la la la la la la

T. oh pep - per - mint freck - les, la la la

B. la la la la la

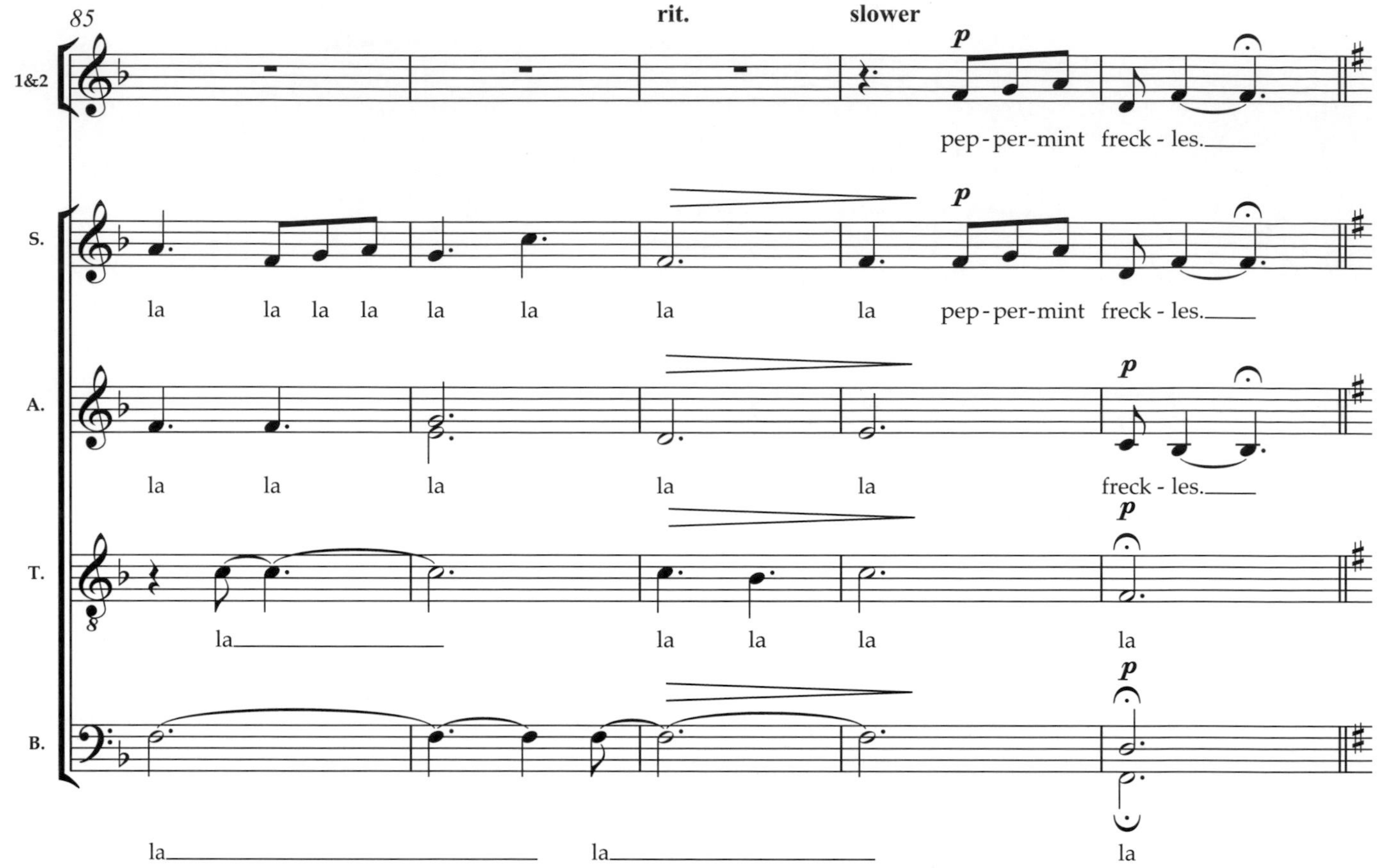

85
rit.
slower
1&2
pep-per-mint freck-les.
S.
la la la la la la la la pep-per-mint freck-les.
A.
la la la la la freck-les.
T.
la la la la la
B.
la la la

4b

6am (Lutra lutra - the otter)

Radiant and dancing ♩ = *c.*144

S. 1
I am Lu-tra lu-tra, I am Lu-tra lu-tra, Lu-tra lu-tra,
A. 1
I am Lu-tra lu-tra, I am Lu-tra lu-tra, Lu-tra lu-tra,
CHOIR 1
T. 1
I am Lu-tra lu-tra, I am Lu-tra lu-tra, Lu-tra
B. 1
I am Lu-tra lu-tra, Lu-tra lu-tra,

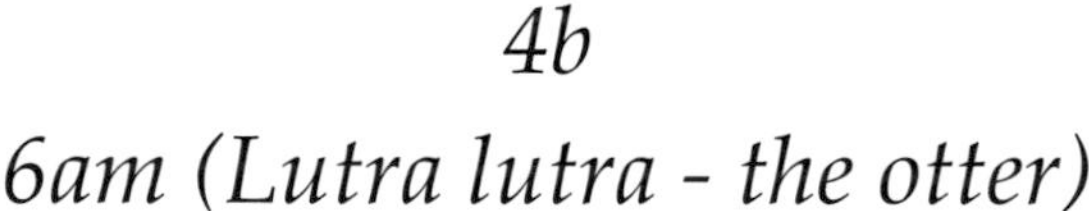

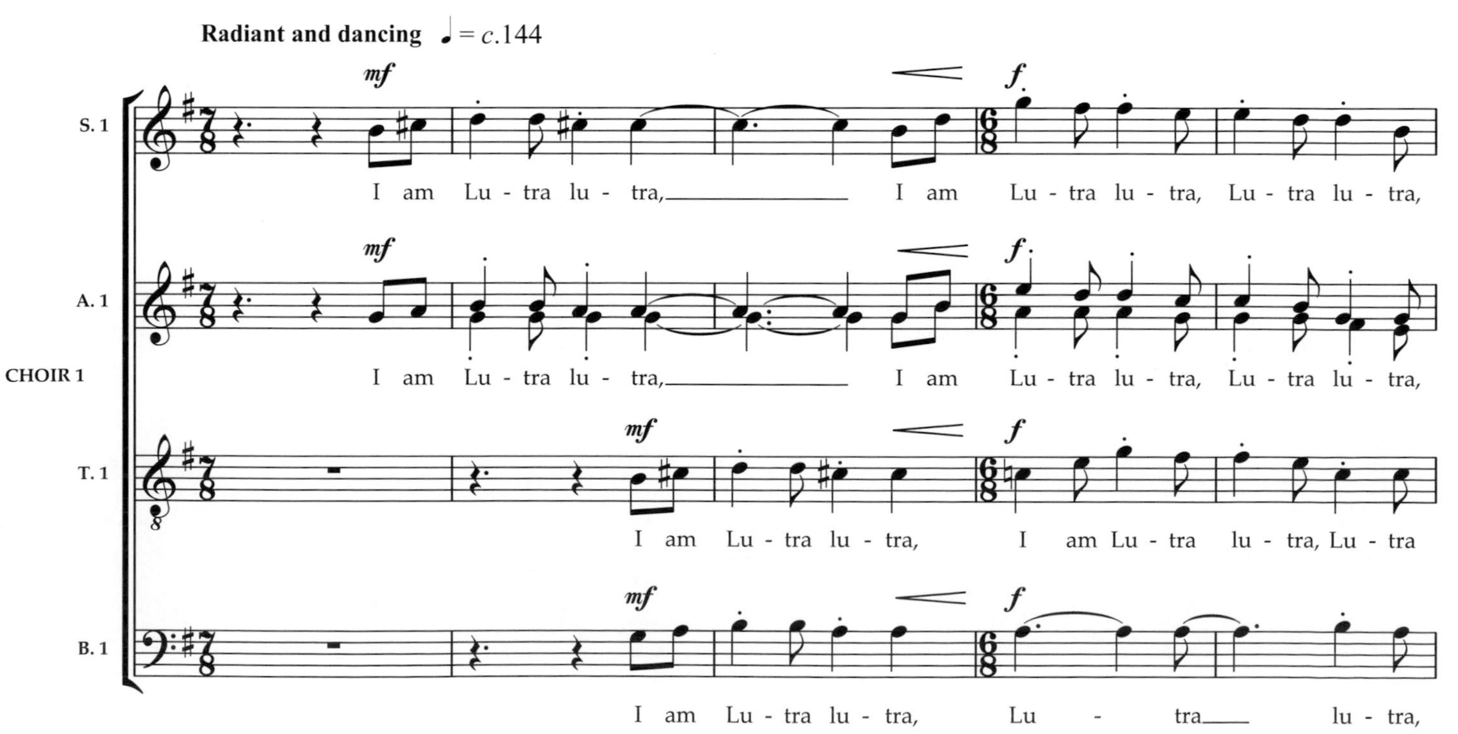

6
S. 1
A. 1
T. 1
B. 1
dim.
mp
mf
Lu - tra. At dawn I walked down to the
Lu - tra. At dawn I walked down to the
lu - tra. Dawn walked down, at
lu - tra. Dawn walked down, at
11
ri - ver; in rolls and spills and rip-ples of fresh light a
ri - ver; in rolls and spills and rip-ples of fresh light a
dawn I walked down to the ri - ver; in rolls and spills and rip-ples of fresh
dawn I walked down to the ri - ver; in rolls and spills and rip-ples of fresh
17
loose-limbed ot - ter lost him-self in wa - ter, a loose - limbed ot - ter
loose-limbed ot - ter lost him-self in wa - ter, a loose - limbed ot - ter
light, a loose-limbed, loose-limbed ot - ter lost him-self in wa - ter, a loose-limbed ot - ter
light a loose-limbed ot - ter lost him-self in wa - ter, a loose-limbed ot - ter

22
dim.
mp
S. 1
lost him-self in wa - ter: I am Lu-tra lu - tra, the cat who swims for
A. 1
lost him-self in wa - ter: I am Lu-tra lu - tra, the cat who swims for
T. 1
lost him-self in, in wa - ter: Lu - tra, I am Lu-tra lu - tra, the
B. 1
lost him-self in, in wa - ter: Lu - tra, I am Lu-tra lu - tra, the
28
mf
S. 1
fish, I am Lu-tra lu - tra, the cat who swims for fish.
A. 1
fish, I am Lu-tra lu - tra, the cat who swims for fish.
T. 1
cat who swims for fish, Lu - tra, I am Lu-tra lu - tra, the cat who swims for
B. 1
cat who swims for fish, Lu - tra, I am Lu-tra lu - tra, the cat who swims for
33
f
S. 1
I am slen - der and lithe and thrive in a long romp. I'm a
A. 1
I am slen - der and lithe and thrive in a long romp. I'm a
T. 1
fish, I am slen - der and lithe and thrive in a long romp. I'm a
B. 1
fish, I am slen - der and lithe and thrive in a long romp. I'm a

38
S. 1
curl, a flip, a slip - p'ry slink, a slosh. I am Lu - tra lu - tra,
A. 1
curl, a flip, a slip - p'ry slink, a slip - p'ry slink, a slosh. I am Lu - tra lu - tra,
T. 1
curl, a curl, a flip, a slip - p'ry slink, a slosh. I am
B. 1
curl, a curl, a flip, a slip - p'ry slink, a slosh. I am
mf
43
S. 1
I am Lu - tra lu - tra, Lu - tra, Lu - tra, Lu - tra. And I
A. 1
I am Lu - tra lu - tra, Lu - tra lu - tra, Lu - tra. And I
T. 1
Lu - tra lu - tra, I am Lu - tra lu - tra, Lu - tra lu - tra.
B. 1
Lu - tra lu - tra, Lu - tra lu - tra, lu - tra.
f
dim.
mp
mf
49
S. 1
found I was flowed through and flowed in - to, as if I swam in a
A. 1
found I was flowed through and flowed in - to, as if I swam in a
T. 1
I was flowed through, and I found I was flowed through and flowed in - to,
B. 1
I was flowed through, and I found I was flowed through and flowed in - to,
mp

54
S. 1
A. 1
T. 1
B. 1
mf
ri - ver of pure light filled with the green breath of a day's be -
ri - ver of pure light filled with the green breath of a day's be -
as if I swam in a ri - ver of pure light, the green breath of a days, the
as if I swam in a ri - ver of pure light, filled with the
59
dim.
-gin - ning, filled with the green breath of a day's be - gin - ning.
-gin - ning, filled with the green breath of a day's be - gin - ning.
breath of a day's be-gin-ning, filled with the green breath of a day's be -
breath of a day's be-gin-ning, filled with the green breath of a day's be -
64
mp
I am Lu - tra lu - tra, the dog who barks in
I am Lu - tra lu - tra, the dog who barks in
-gin - ning. Lu - tra, I am Lu - tra lu - tra, the
-gin - ning. Lu - tra, I am Lu - tra lu - tra, the

68
S. 1
A. 1
T. 1
B. 1
mf
dark - ness, I am Lu - tra lu - tra, the dog who barks in dark - ness.
dog who barks in dark - ness, Lu - tra, I am Lu - tra lu - tra, the dog who barks in
dog who barks in dar - ness, Lu - tra, I am Lu - tra lu - tra, the dog who barks in
73
f
I am laugh - ter in wa - ter, in wa - ter, o - ver -
dark - ness. I am laugh - ter in wa - ter, in wa - ter, o - ver -
77
- flow - ing. My pups, my pups are more of me to - mor - row.
- flow - ing. My pups, my pups are more of me, are more of me to -
- flow - ing. My pups are more of me, are more of me to -
- flow - ing. My pups are more of me, are more of me to -

81
mf
f dim.
S. 1
I am Lu - tra lu - tra, I am Lu - tra lu - tra, Lu - tra lu - tra,
A. 1
-mor - row. I am Lu - tra lu - tra, I am Lu - tra lu - tra, Lu - tra lu - tra,
T. 1
-mor - row. I am Lu - tra lu - tra, I am Lu - tra lu - tra, Lu - tra
B. 1
-mor - row. I am Lu - tra lu - tra, Lu - tra lu - tra,

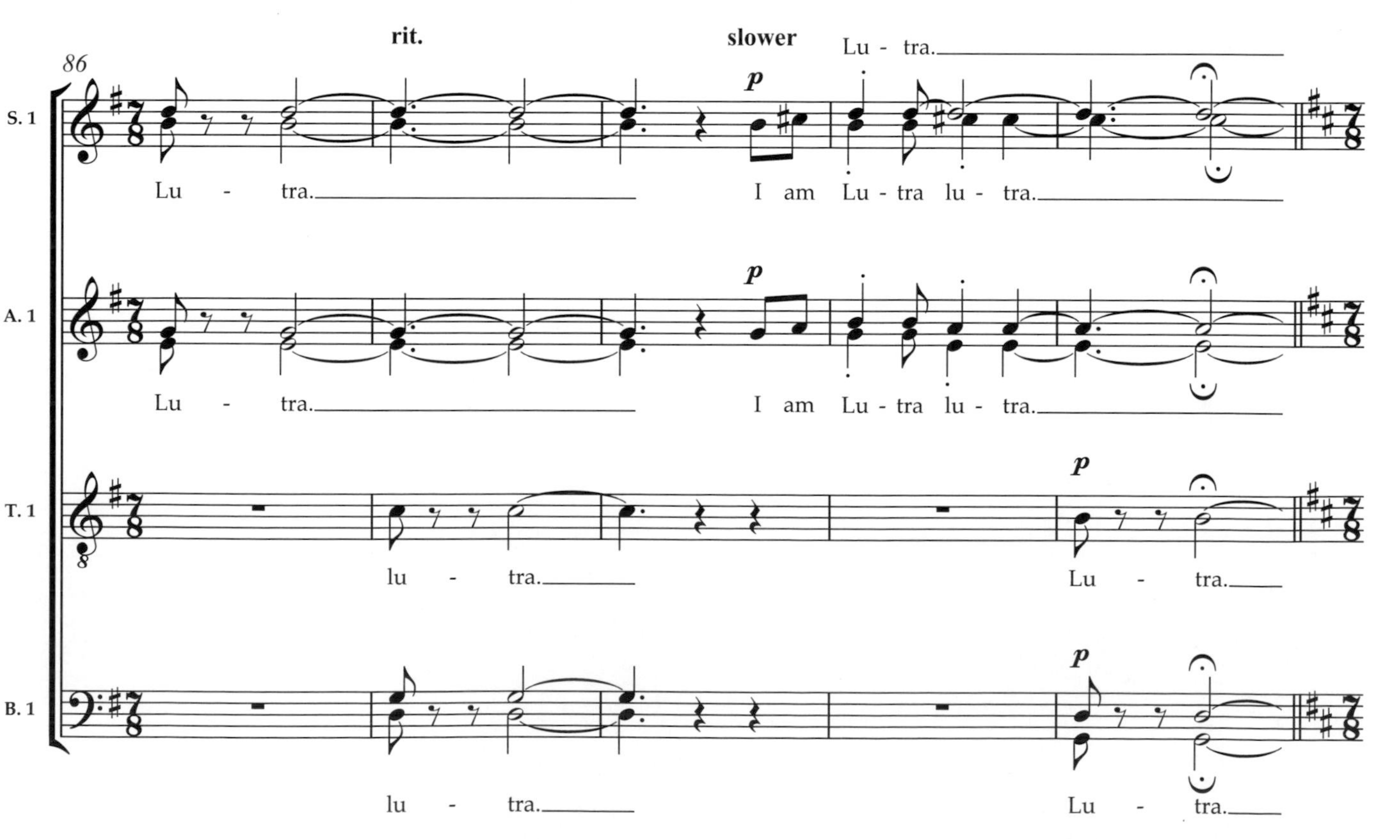
86
rit.
slower
p
S. 1
Lu - tra.
Lu - tra. I am Lu - tra lu - tra.
A. 1
Lu - tra. I am Lu - tra lu - tra.
T. 1
lu - tra. Lu - tra.
B. 1
lu - tra. Lu - tra.

4c
Perhaps

Gentle but with a positive air ♩ = c.84
mp
S.
One foot in win-ter the o-ther in spring, one foot in win-ter the o-ther in spring, one foot in win-ter the
mp
A.
One foot in win-ter the o-ther in spring, one foot in win-ter the o-ther in spring, one foot in win-ter the
CHAMBER CHOIR
T.
mp
B.
oo
S. 1
A. 1
CHOIR 1
T. 1
B. 1
S. 2
A. 2
CHOIR 2
T. 2
B. 2

6
S.
o-ther in spring, one foot in win-ter the o-ther in spring, one foot in win - ter the o-ther in spring,
A.
o-ther in spring, one foot in win-ter the o-ther in spring, one foot in win - ter the o-ther in spring,
T.
mp
oo oo
B.
oo oo
S. 1
p dolce
We're stand-ing with one foot in win - ter
A. 1
p dolce
We're stand-ing with one foot in win - ter
T. 1
p dolce
We're stand-ing with one foot in win - ter
B. 1
p dolce
We're stand-ing with one foot in win - ter
S. 2
p
Ah
A. 2
T. 2
B. 2

11
S.
one foot in win - ter the o - ther in spring, one foot in win - ter the o - ther in spring,
A.
one foot in win - ter the o - ther in spring, one foot in win - ter the o - ther in spring,
T.
oo oo
B.
oo oo
S. 1
and the o - ther in spring.
A. 1
and the o - ther in spring.
T. 1
and the o - ther in spring.
B. 1
and the o - ther in spring.
S. 2
p dolce
We're stand - ing with one foot in win - ter
A. 2
p dolce
We're stand - ing with one foot in win - ter
T. 2
p dolce
We're stand - ing with one foot in win - ter
B. 2
p dolce
We're stand - ing with one foot in win - ter

15
p
S.
one foot in win - ter the o - ther in spring,
ah
A.
one foot in win - ter the o - ther in spring, one foot in win - ter the o - ther in spring,
T.
one foot in win - ter the o - ther in spring,
ah ah ah
B.
oo ah
mp
S. 1
Turn-ing the clocks for - ward makes the
A. 1
Turn-ing the clocks for - ward makes the
T. 1
Turn-ing the clocks for - ward makes the
B. 1
Turn-ing the clocks for - ward makes the
S. 2
and the o - ther in spring. Ah
A. 2
and the o - ther in spring.
T. 2
and the o - ther in spring. Ah
B. 2
and the o - ther in spring.

19
S.
one foot in win - ter the o - ther in spring,
A.
one foot in win - ter the o - ther in spring, one foot in win - ter the o - ther in spring,
T.
one foot in win - ter the o - ther in spring, ah
uh uh
B.
ah ah ah ah
S. 1
p
stars_ grow old - er, old - er by an hour.
A. 1
p
stars_ grow old - er, old - er by an hour.
T. 1
p
stars_ grow old - er, old - er by an hour.
B. 1
p
stars_ grow old - er, old - er by an hour.
S. 2
ah
A. 2
T. 2
ah
B. 2

23
S.
A.
T.
B.
one foot in win - ter the o - ther in spring, one foot in win - ter the o - ther in spring,
one foot in win - ter the o - ther in spring, one foot in win - ter the o - ther in spring,
mp
ah ah
ah
S. 1
A. 1
T. 1
B. 1
p
In the mid-dle of dark and dark we take our
In the mid-dle of dark and dark we take our
In the mid-dle of dark and
In the mid-dle of dark and
S. 2
A. 2
T. 2
B. 2
Ah
win - ter,
win - ter,
dark, dark, dark,
dark, dark, dark,

27
S.
one foot in win - ter the o - ther in spring, one foot in win - ter the o - ther in spring,
A.
one foot in win - ter the o - ther in spring, one foot in win - ter the o - ther in spring,
T.
ah ah
B.
ah ah
S. 1
time. win - ter,
A. 1
time. win - ter,
T. 1
dark we take our time. dark, dark, dark,
B. 1
dark we take our time. dark, dark, dark,
S. 2
p
In the mid-dle of dark and dark we take our
A. 2
p
In the mid-dle of dark and dark we take our
T. 2
dark, dark, dark,
p
In the mid-dle of dark and
B. 2
dark, dark, dark,
p
In the mid-dle of dark and

31
S.
one foot in win - ter the o - ther in spring,
ah
A.
one foot in win - ter the o - ther in spring, one foot in win - ter the o - ther in spring,
T.
one foot in win - ter the o - ther in spring,
ah ah ah
B.
ah ah
S. 1
As if we stood on a see - saw and
A. 1
As if we stood on a see - saw and
T. 1
dark, dark, dark, As if we stood on a
B. 1
dark, dark, dark, As if we stood on a
S. 2
time. Ah
A. 2
time.
T. 2
dark we take our time. Ah
B. 2
dark we take our time.

35
S.
one foot in win - ter the o - ther in spring,
A.
one foot in win - ter the o - ther in spring, one foot in win - ter the o - ther in spring,
T.
one foot in win - ter the o - ther in spring, ah
ah
B.
ah ah ah
S. 1
felt the sum - mer tilt its weight of light.
A. 1
felt the sum - mer tilt its weight of light.
T. 1
see - saw and felt the sum - mer tilt its weight of light.
B. 1
see - saw and felt the sum - mer tilt its weight of light.
S. 2
ah
A. 2
T. 2
ah
B. 2

39
S.
one foot in win - ter the o - ther in spring,
A.
one foot in win - ter the o - ther in spring,
T.
B.
ah
S. 1
mp cresc.
Win-ter's a cloud in the shape of a ques-tion a -
A. 1
mp cresc.
Win-ter's a cloud in the shape of a ques-tion a -
T. 1
mp cresc.
Win - ter, win-ter shape of a
B. 1
mp cresc.
Win - ter the shape of a
S. 2
Ah
mp cresc.
Win-ter's a cloud in the
A. 2
mp cresc.
Win-ter's a cloud in the
T. 2
mp cresc.
Win-ter's a cloud, a
B. 2
mp cresc.
Win-ter's a cloud, a

43
S.
mp cresc.
mf
It smears the mor - ning sky,
A.
It smears the mor - ning, mor - ning sky,
T.
It smears the mor - ning, mor - ning sky,
B.
It smears the mor - ning, mor - ning sky,
S. 1
-bove us, and will not fade un - til we have found an
A. 1
-bove us, a - bove us, and will not fade un - til we have found an
T. 1
ques - tion, and will not fade till we have found an
B. 1
ques - tion, and will not fade till we have found an
S. 2
shape of a ques-tion a - bove us, and will not fade un -
A. 2
shape of a ques-tion, a ques - tion a - bove us, and will not fade un -
T. 2
cloud in the shape of a ques - tion, and will not
B. 2
cloud in the shape of a ques - tion, and will not

47
S.
and will not, will not fade,
A.
and will not, will not fade,
T.
and will not, will not fade,
B.
and will not, will not fade,
S. 1
an - swer. The see - saw lifts and dips as we won - der
A. 1
an-swer, an an - swer. The see - saw lifts and dips as we won - der
T. 1
an - swer. The see - saw lifts and dips as we
B. 1
an - swer. The see - saw lifts and dips as we
S. 2
-til we have found an an - swer. The see - saw lifts and
A. 2
-til we have found, have found an an - swer. The see - saw lifts and
T. 2
fade un - til we have found an an - swer. The see - saw lifts and
B. 2
fade un - til we have found an an - swer. The see - saw lifts and
f

51
S.
ff
we won - der,
A.
ff
we won - der,
T.
ff
we won - der,
B.
ff
we won - der,
S. 1
ff
to our - selves, we won - der to our - selves, we won - der to our
A. 1
ff
to our - selves, we won - der to our - selves, we won - der to our
T. 1
ff
won - der, we won - der to our - selves, we won - der to our - selves, we
B. 1
ff
won - der, we won - der to our - selves, we won - der to our - selves, we
S. 2
ff
dips as we won - der to our - selves, we won - der to our - selves, we
A. 2
ff
dips as we won - der to, to our - selves, we won - der to our - selves, we
T. 2
ff
dips, we won - der to our - selves, we won - der to our - selves, we
B. 2
ff
dips, we won - der to our - selves, we won - der to our - selves, we

56
S.
A.
T.
B.
sub. mp
we won - der: can we learn how to live with this world? Can we learn how to live with this world?
mp
oo
oo
S. 1
A. 1
T. 1
B. 1
molto dim.
-selves, our - selves:
-selves, our - selves, our - selves:
won-der to our - selves, our - selves:
won-der to our - selves:
S. 2
A. 2
T. 2
B. 2
won-der to our - selves, our - selves:
won - der to our - selves, our - selves:
won - der to our - selves:

1st TIME: mp
2nd TIME: p
3rd TIME: pp
61
Spoken - all at different times and at different pitches
CHILDREN'S CHOIR
Per-haps, per-haps.
S.
Can we learn how to live with this world? Can we learn how to live with this world?
A.
Can we learn how to live with this world? Can we learn how to live with this world?
T.
oo oo
B.
oo oo
S. 1
The spar-rows sing:
A. 1
The spar-rows sing:
T. 1
The spar-rows sing:
B. 1
The spar-rows sing:
S. 2
The spar-rows sing: Ah
A. 2
The spar-rows sing:
T. 2
The spar-rows sing: world, world,
B. 2
The spar-rows sing: world, world,

65
1.2.
3.
S.
Can we learn how to live with this world?
Can we learn how to live with this world?
A.
Can we learn how to live with this world?
Can we learn how to live with this world?
T.
oo
(oo)
oo
oo
B.
oo
(oo)
oo
S. 1
Ah
(ah)
A. 1
T. 1
world,
world,
B. 1
world,
world,
S. 2
A. 2
T. 2
B. 2

rit.
slow
69
S.
Can we learn how to live with this world, live with this world, this world?
A.
Can we learn how to live with this world, live with this world, this world?
T.
oo oo oo this world?
B.
oo oo oo this world?
S. 1
ah ah this world?
A. 1
this world?
T. 1
world, world, this world?
B. 1
world, world, this world?
S. 2
this world?
A. 2
this world?
T. 2
this world?
B. 2
this world?